Obamageddon

The Culmination of the Progressive

Looting of America

Bruce Kreitler

Dedicated to my Father, Clark Franklin Kreitler 1930—2010, a True American Hero

-LTC, United States Army (Regular Army) 1952—1972-

A nation can survive its fools, and even the ambitious. But it cannot survive treason from within. An enemy at the gates is less formidable, for he is known and carries his banner openly. But the traitor moves amongst those within the gate freely, his sly whispers rustling through all the alleys, heard in the very halls of government itself. For the traitor appears not a traitor; he speaks in accents familiar to his victims, and he wears their face and their arguments, he appeals to the baseness that lies deep in the hearts of all men. He rots the soul of a nation, he works secretly and unknown in the night to undermine the pillars of the city, he infects the body politic so that it can no longer resist. A murderer is less to fear. The traitor is the plague.
-Cicero, circa 50 B.C.

TABLE OF CONTENTS

Preface

In my opinion the United States of America now faces as great a danger to its existence as it has at any time in the past. While in our long history we have been through many dark and dangerous times, we have faced no enemy or problem like the issues before us now. As bad and divisive as the Civil War was, we survived it (albeit at a soul-numbing cost in lives lost or destroyed), and it did finally rid us of the national shame of slavery.

I honestly think that the interior struggle that we are facing now carries the seeds of our ultimate destruction if we don't come together and solve the problems before us. And we won't go down alone either; if the shining beacon of truth and justice that is the United States succumbs, there will not be any other country left to take up the struggle for religious freedom and human rights. The few countries that share our beliefs will rise or fall with us.

The republic that our founding fathers created, coupled with the capitalistic economics that we have enjoyed, has been the best human society ever seen on the face of the earth. And don't let the left fool you about that. Democracy coupled with capitalism and our Christian heritage has improved the human condition beyond anything ever envisioned by our forefathers. Our enemies realize this, so they never miss an opportunity to try and convince us that capitalism is bad and the United States isn't a Christian nation.

The founding fathers fought the Revolutionary War and struggled through the Articles of Confederation to our Constitution. They and their children fought the War of 1812, and their children and grandchildren fought the Civil War. Our great grandfathers fought in the First World War, and our grandparents and parents fought tyranny and oppression in World War II. Our parent's generation struggled through the Vietnam War and all the social unrest that went with it. Now, we are faced with a different kind of threat that is much worse than anything that has gone before. The danger to our republic and the rest of the world is insidious betrayal from within. The ultimate goals of this group will result in the economic enslavement and religious repression of the citizens of the United States. As goes the United States, so will go our allies and like-minded countries.

Over many years, the enemies of our republic have evolved and developed the methods they use to permeate our political system and control us. The battle before us now is not a fight between armies for the physical control of the United States; what we are facing is a battle of ideas and philosophy for the control of the federal government and hence the freedom of the citizens of the United States of America.

As with all the people who struggled and triumphed before us, we are reluctant, unready, woefully unprepared, and would really prefer to just be left alone so we can mind our own business and just go on with our normal lives. Unfortunately, just as with our predecessors, we are here, the time is now, and the only choice left to us is which side we are on.

What we have now is a battle for the control and direction of the national government; if we don't get this right, and soon, we could very easily learn the difference between a "soft tyranny," and outright government repression.

Ready or not, the struggle for the economic and religious freedom of Western Civilization in general and the United States in particular is upon us, and the only decision left to you is—are you for or against?

Who am I?

Who am I to write a book like this? Well, before I start on who I am, let me tell you who I'm not.

I'm not a professional political commentator. I have no education in politics beyond my high school government class, and I'm not sure if the woman who taught it was a liberal or conservative, but I will tell you that she did her level best to teach a class of inattentive teenagers as much about American government, and it's history, as well as our part in its continuance as she could. At the time, I gave little thought to her efforts other than to make sure that I passed the class so I could graduate. With thirty plus years of hindsight, I think she took a difficult job and did what she could to teach all of us as much as possible.

I don't move in a circle of movers and shakers. I know, or at least know who a lot of those people in my area are, not because I'm one of them but due to the fact that I meet a lot of them in the course of everyday business and life.

I very seldom wear a suit. One of my goals in life is to inhabit a suit as infrequently as possible. Instead, I spend most of my waking hours in jeans, and I'm perfectly happy with that arrangement.

I'm not a financial guru, as evidenced by the fact that I'm not rich and I have to watch my money very carefully. I doubt that I'm alone in this; I think that both the people with less money than I and the ones that I personally would consider to be wealthy also have to pay the same attention to their finances.

I have never served in any of our armed forces nor have I ever held any kind of government job, but as my father was a career military officer, I am familiar with life on military reservations as a military dependant.

In short, I have no claim to being a professional commentator, policy wonk, financial guru, or government insider. I just feel that what is going on in our country now has become so obvious, that it has become a case of the emperor's new clothes and it is past time for somebody to stand up and say, "The emperor has no clothes!" (I don't think that is the actual quote from the story, but it is what we are used to hearing.) What is surprising to me is that somebody who is a professional commentator, political observer, or financial sage hasn't come out with something like this book. Many of them have spoken of or alluded to a lot of what I'm writing about, but so far I haven't happened across any single source that doesn't beat around the bush rather than just coming out and putting the whole thing together.

As far as my education goes, I am definitely a product of the school of hard knocks. This has a lot more to do with my own mistakes than it has to do with a lack of opportunity or any abuse afflicted on me by someone else. In spite of my tendency (which I share with a lot of people) to not make the exactly right decision at every turn, the capitalistic, democratic society that up to this point has been the United States has always allowed me another chance, as long as I'm willing to pursue it. Despite the saying that opportunity only knocks once, the fact is our forefathers founded a country where opportunity knocks all the time.

These plentiful opportunities that are open to all, are a large part of how most people have become successful; and it is our duty to both ourselves and future generations to preserve that system of opportunity. I'll be right up front here, I have a vested interest in this preservation, I hope to make use of the system to better myself economically. Therefore, I'm very interested in preserving the economic and political structure that will allow me to do that.

I have traveled a lot and spent quite a bit of time in a country where the rulers of that country have stifled both economic opportunity and personal freedom. That country is one of those places that when the police, or whatever type of guard you might be dealing with held out his (that's not a gender mistake—it was always a male) hand and said, "Papers," you had better have them. This same country also had at that time, and still has today, religious police that were a separate force that as nearly as I could tell appointed themselves and did not answer to anybody. So when I write further in this book about religious freedom, I have been places where religious intolerance was the law of the land and religious freedom did not (and still doesn't) exist. Religious freedom is one more thing that we must preserve in our country. Maybe the time that I spent in places like I described makes me a little more sensitive to the rapid erosion of our liberty and freedom that is part and parcel of the dismantling of our capitalist society.

I am a Christian and believe that the United States was founded on Christian principles; the Claptrap the left puts out about us not being a Christian nation is not only untrue, it is just one more facet of the progressives attack on our basic principles.

I also believe very firmly in religious freedom, what religion my neighbors chooses to practice is strictly up to them as long as that practice does not interfere with anybody else's rights or break any laws. I do think we can safely say that people who blow themselves and any bystanders to pieces are creating a problem and need to be dealt with. I feel no need to "reach out" to these people or try to "understand where they are coming from." I'm also not concerned with what their motivations are. I do believe that it is the duty of our federal government to deal very firmly with these people when they catch them, which does not include extending them our own constitutional protections.

Isn't it ironic that at a time when the constitutional protections that the average American citizen should have are under attack by the federal government, this same government is trying (successfully) to extend constitutional rights that are being taken away from actual Americans to terrorist prisoners? Maybe we are going about trying to rein in the federal government all wrong. Maybe we should have Somali pirates and Afghani members of Al Qaeda take test cases to the Supreme Court for us. Judging by current events, they probably would get more sympathy from the left than a conservative or just plain American citizen would.

Without a doubt, I would be labeled as being pro states' rights. I do believe that most of what the federal government has taken on itself are not only powers that really belong to the states, but I additionally think that most of what the federal government has worked its fingers into are things that would be better handled at the state level.

I think this way not because I consider state governments to be better, more efficient, or necessarily the best organizations to get things done.

I want more of our governing done at the state level and less by the federal government for three reasons. One, constitutionally, the federal government has just flat out taken things upon itself that are not federal matters. In short, I feel that a lot of what the federal government is doing is unconstitutional and must be stopped or returned to the states for that reason. Secondly, state governments are closer to their citizens. Being closer to the populace means more feedback, more citizen participation, and, this is really important, more day-to-day observation of government matters by the actual taxpayer/voters. Third, the liberal progressives have permeated the federal government and grown it to a level of abuse that previously I would have said couldn't be topped. However, now Obama has come along and pushed the abuses of the federal government to formerly unbelievable heights. Any power that we can take away from this overweening federal monster and give back to the states would have to be a good thing; after all, if nothing else, the states aren't going to do a worse job of management—well, maybe except for California.

My wife and I own a small company that we have organized as a subchapter S corporation. I know that as far as a liberal would be concerned, that automatically makes me an independently wealthy source of federal revenue. Additionally, the fact that we own one of those "evil" corporations just makes us a juicy double-taxation target that fully deserves any treatment that the fed decides to subject us to. After all, we must be abusing some poor workers to further our own selfish aims.

The fact of the matter is that the last two years have been a very rough time to be business owners. I enjoy what we do, but it takes all of my attention to keep my employees and myself in work and getting an income. Truthfully, in 2010, my employees made much more money than I did. I hope that we do better in 2011, but I can guarantee you that I'm not waiting around for the government to help me improve. In fact, a lot of what makes it hard to run an ethical, profitable business is direct interference from government entities and indirect problems caused by liberal policies.

The labor force in this country is declining rapidly, and I think that can be traced directly back to liberal policies. Just to name a few, tacit encouragement of illegal immigration, the dumbing down of the curriculum and lack of discipline that exists in our public schools, unemployment benefits that are too easy to obtain, subsidizing the breakup of poor families, and the general watering down of the work ethic and personal responsibility that are both the result and the actual goal of the progressive nanny state entitlement programs. This gradual destruction of our labor force alone will eventually turn us into a third world country; and it is a direct result of the federal government's progressive policies, yet little is said about it, and the liberals continue to grow their destructive programs unchecked.

Since I am a business owner and I deal with our labor force on a daily basis, this dissolution of one of our greatest assets (the willingness and ability to work) catches my attention. I am not sitting in a comfortable chair in Washington, DC, (seat of the federal government and coincidentally, or maybe not, a city with one of the higher murder rates in the United States) arguing about the effects of the liberal policies. As a working, taxpaying, business owner, I am dealing with the consequences of progressivism every day. That gives me both a lot of personal experience with the human waste created by the liberals and a huge amount of frustration. Hence, this book.

This erosion of ethics, morality, family values, and public education, along with the explosion of public debt is definitely not what the left has been promising to deliver with their "progressive" programs, but all of these problems can indeed be laid at the feet of the "nanny state."

As I have already said, I have no academic or commentary background that would give me legitimacy for a work like this. What I do have is the fact that I am one more citizen who is forced to deal with the effects of the progressive programs coming out of Washington. When I interview a potential worker who doesn't have a driver's license, can't read or write, has a criminal record, and basically doesn't even realize that dressing neatly and speaking politely is an important part of a job interview, I have to wonder about the conditions that exist in our country that can produce a large pool of people like that one. By the way, I'm not speaking hypothetically; I do have people contact me looking for work who are just as I have described. My experience is that our population is growing, but our qualified labor pool is shrinking. If you think that I'm incorrect about that, do some digging on your own; you will be shocked at what you find.

I have a lifelong interest in reading history, and that has possibly given me a little different slant on why people (societies and politicians) do things. Unlike many people who go with the old saw, that if we don't learn history we are doomed to repeat it, I think that looking at things from the perspective of history just gives a better understanding of what drove the actions and decisions of the people involved. This way of thinking is just another tool to help decipher what is going on in the here and now.

So in two hundred years, do we want people looking back at how we handled ourselves and saying, "Why couldn't they see what was happening to them?" Instead, how about fifty years from now, our grandchildren are reading books about how we gathered ourselves together and saved our country from destruction? The choice is ours.

So to sum up, the problems that have been created by more than half a century of "socially progressive" programs that have now led us to Barack Hussein Obama have become so large and so obvious that even a guy like me with no background in reporting, commentary, politics, or even a college degree can see them. So instead of thinking, "Who am I to write this book?" I'm wondering instead why somebody else with more credentials and better political or economic standing hasn't already written it.

Who Are the Enemies of Our Republic?

Okay, who exactly are the enemies of our republic, why are they enemies, and what do they want to accomplish?

Since the republic that is the United States is a prosperous, capitalist society that believes in human rights, freedom of religion, and has a Christian heritage, we have picked up a lot of enemies along the way.

We have fought, and continue to fight, against fascism, colonialism, piracy, communism, genocide, religious fundamentalism, dictatorships, and for basic human rights both on the battlefield and in the economic arena. Castro's Cuba exists solely because we have made a decision to not invade his country. Rightly, or wrongly, Castro is there not because of anything that he has done, but because of something that we have decided not to do.

Naturally this willingness to stand up against these things while supporting God-given human rights has made us unpopular with genocidal regimes, communists, religious fundamentalists, dictators, governments that would like to wipe out a class of people, pirates and the countries that harbor them, fascists, and just generally any people that would like to unilaterally rule over other people with no regard for human rights. I'm proud to live in a country that has managed to pick up that set of enemies.

Nevertheless, all of the outside opponents of our republic and our way of life that we can face head-on, we have either defeated, or driven back. To outsiders America may seem very divided, but when faced with an outside foe, we manage to come together and defeat them.

In my opinion, the two most dangerous enemies that we face at this point in time are liberals and religious fundamentalists; since the Buddhist or Hindu religious fundamentalists have not been much of a problem lately, I, of course, mean the Muslim religious fundamentalists that have declared holy war or jihad on Western civilization. As much as I have been told (I bet I've spoken with more Muslims than almost anybody reading this book) that Islam is a religion of peace and love, I don't see it.

Muslim religious fundamentalists have caused, and are causing, us a lot of trouble. These people are creating violence wherever they exist in the world and are a problem for us and a lot of other countries. However; even as big an issue as they are, frankly, if we had our domestic house in order and order was coupled with competent leadership, the fundamentalist issue would be much easier to resolve.

That single biggest enemy that we face in this day and age is the people in our government who claim to be "progressives." Most of the rest of us would call them liberals, libs, the left, or leftists and for clarity's sake, I'm going to refer to them in that manner, but these progressives are working toward our destruction from the inside.

I don't think that the dissolution of the United States is their actual aim; in fact most of them would be shocked if they were accused of it. However, whether or not they are doing it on purpose, the fact remains that liberal policies coupled with runaway entitlement spending have seriously weakened us, and we are now vulnerable to our enemies. Intentionally or not, the cumulative effects of social progressiveness and unbridled spending have brought us to this potentially disastrous state of affairs.

Before I continue, I want to make some distinctions. When I say that the liberals are our enemy, and are working toward our destruction, I am not talking about the average person who thinks of himself as liberal or politically correct or socially progressive or kinder and gentler than the nasty conservatives or whatever label these misguided citizens who conservatives call liberals would like to attach to themselves. They are part of the problem, but not intentionally.

I'm additionally not picking on Democrats, or Republicans. This book concerns liberal and conservative which are beliefs, not Republicans or Democrats, which are political affiliations. Granted, most liberals are going to be Democrats and most conservatives will be Republicans, but the Republicans are not all conservatives and the Democrats are not all liberals.

In the few places in this book where I do use the labels Democrat and Republican, I will only be using those terms as the people under discussion apply them to themselves or what they are talking about.

Leaving out the Muslim religious fundamentalists for a moment, as I see it, there are three main groups of people that have helped to bring us to our present position and are contributing to our present difficulties.

I think that the group of career federal politicians who label themselves as liberals or progressives, to hide their true agenda, are the people who got us where we are now; and yes, I am well aware that they couldn't have done it without cooperation from other politicians of both parties. I think that their lust for power, money, and control has grown the federal government into the power-grabbing, money-sucking, freedom-stifling monstrosity that it is today. I additionally think that they have done this without regard for anything other than furthering their personal gains. What this personal gain has done to our country and the citizens of this great republic does not enter into their thinking, nor influence their decisions. These are the people that we must weed out of our government.

These people aren't even hard to find. They hide right out in the open. If you simply look at voting records instead of listening to what they say, it is pretty easy to see who is trying to stand up for our country and who is just trying to line their pockets. I will admit, that every once in awhile if you listen to shady politicians, they will accidentally tell you what they really mean. Either that or say something that tells you everything you need to know about them. For instance, on the ninth of January 2010, I heard Harry Reid say on Meet the Press that social security is not a problem because it is fully funded for the next forty years. Now I know that Reid couldn't have been trying to convince himself of that because he should know better. So I have to assume that he expected the people listening to him to swallow that whopper. Now, I, of course, already have a fully formed opinion of Harry Reid, but if I had not previously made up my mind, listening to that statement would have given me all the information I needed to decide where Harry Reid stands in the struggle to reform our federal government.

While the power-seeking politicians who are ruining us aren't that hard to find, they would not be able to do this without the ability to be voted into and remain in office. We may come to a time in the future when the individual votes of citizens are not important, but for now, that is how these people get the power that they so crave.

They do this by convincing two main groups of people that voting for them is a good thing. These two types of citizens are the liberals, as you would expect, and surprisingly, the people who call themselves moderates or independents.

The citizens who call themselves moderates or independents will generally tell you that they vote for the person running without regard to political affiliation. Dishonest politicians make good use of these people. Since an honest or citizen-legislator type of politician is generally going to let people know where they really stand on issues, they can easily turn away these centrist voters. A dishonest politician, on the other hand is not going to have any trouble telling the independent voters exactly what those uncommitted people want to hear. Couple that with the power of incumbency, and it's easy to see how the dishonest career politicians stay in power as long as they do. (Can you say Robert Byrd?)

I'm sure that people who consider themselves moderates would be upset to discover that I have labeled them as being part of the problem, but the fact of the matter is their middle-of-the-road politics and wish for bipartisanship is contributing to the dismantling of our republic.

Of course, the base the so-called "progressive" politician relies on is only partially composed of the voters who label themselves as liberals or progressives. The base liberal voting bloc is actually made up of two main groups. One group is the people that either are recipients of government money through entitlement programs or in some other way depend on the federal government for their income. Naturally, this group is very hesitant to change the status quo. In fact, these people become quite vocal anytime that their entitlements or income is threatened. This collection of voters certainly includes the poor people that receive money and benefits through the government social programs.

The second set of people that make up the liberal voting bloc are the citizens that don't rely on the fed for a living, but class themselves as liberals or social progressives. These are the people that have actually become convinced that liberalism is the way to go. This group thinks that not only do the government programs work, but we have a civic duty to keep them in place, maintain or increase the budgets and generally just stay the course. As far as these people are concerned government confiscating private money and redistributing it among people that aren't willing to earn it is exactly the way to go. When Obama told Joe the plumber, "I think when you spread the wealth around, it's good for everybody," he was speaking to the two biggest groups in his base. First, the ones who want as much taxpayer money and benefits for themselves as they can get, and secondly, the people that want to get that taxpayer money so they can give it to the first group.

The liberal voters who are voting for politicians who will maintain or increase the programs that are funneling money and benefits back to them are voting only to fill their pockets. These people are not interested in the fate of the country and additionally are not interested in how or where the federal government gets the money for these programs. They vote the straight self-interest ticket, and the only way to ever change that would be to somehow convert them from public assistance recipients into taxpayers. Since these people are such dependable liberal voters, the left continues to dole out money and entitlement programs to them but strenuously resists any real effort help these people truly leave public assistance behind them.

As misguided and under informed as I think the average liberal, who is not voting because of self interest, is, I still think that they mean well. They have just allowed themselves to be convinced that the leftist agenda is a good idea. These are the people that are gullible enough to be fooled by the constant barrage of liberal media and the smooth sounding speeches of leftist politicians. For whatever reason, the average liberal seems to have a hard time sorting out facts for themselves.

I'm not going to say that I don't have a bone to pick with liberal citizens, because I do. I think that they need to put off the politically correct brainwashing that makes them think the liberal policies of the federal government are helpful to our society. The fact that the average Democrat can stand behind loonies like Barney Frank, Jesse Jackson, former Senator Ted "Chappaquiddick" Kennedy, Al Gore, Obama, Biden, etc. and actually believe that these people have any good intentions for our republic just sets my teeth on edge.

Just as I am proud of the declared enemies that being a champion of human of rights have garnered our country, if I found myself in a group that contained the people I listed in the previous paragraph, I would automatically change sides. I don't quite get the thinking that would allow somebody to think Sarah Palin is a bad person, and then go pull Barney Frank's leve..., I mean go vote for Barney Frank. I wonder if all of these people are products of our public schools. If they are, I can't make a better argument for abolishing the department of education and returning control of public education to the local school boards.

Regardless of where the self-supporting liberal citizens got their ideas, and how badly they are in need of better education, at least these people actually are well intentioned. What they stand for and how they want to implement it will be, and is, harmful to our republic, but at least they do mean to be helpful. Think of them as well intentioned but not very competent.

The real enemies are the people in our government who are actually implementing all these liberal policies. They are using the voting power of the well-intentioned liberals and any other groups that they can control to further the agenda of more federal money spent, more control of the average citizen, more federal bureaucrats, more borrowing (just part of the spending), and as close to absolute control of all the activity of the United States citizens as they can get.

The difference between the average well-meaning, self labeled, liberal and the people in power that identify themselves as liberals is huge. As I said the average person who likes liberal policies really believes that these programs are going to help people. The reason that they believe that is because the liberal media and the federal government have been telling them for years and years that the liberal agenda is both critically necessary and extremely beneficial. These are the people that when you present them with information showing the harm some of these leftist programs have done (the destruction of the poor black family comes to my mind), they will say something along the lines of "I don't care what you think." Not a very intellectual response, but it is a step above calling you a nazi.

The ultimate goal of the liberals, who are actually in charge, is power, and just for the sake of having that power. Their quest is destroying the United States, but the destruction of the U.S. is not the actual aim. The only goal of these liberals is to be the ruling class. The more federal money that they can control, the more bureaucrats who exercise that authority, and the more individual rights that they can take from the states and states' citizens, the better they like it. The damage they do in getting that power is an incidental result of their power-seeking policies.

I don't see this as some big conspiracy involving a lot of people having clandestine meetings with the intention of working toward the single goal of destroying the United State. I think what is going on is more that we have accumulated a lot of totally unethical power- and money-hungry politicians in one spot (the federal government) who have become very good at manipulating people. How else can you explain Barney Frank (father of the housing market crash) being re-elected?

These liberal politicians only cooperate among themselves as much as they have to so they can remain in office, beyond that, it seems they would and do attack each other when it serves their purposes. The united front that they seem to show is just that—a show. The one and only goal of each of them is more federal dollars and federal employees under their direct, personal control. As they increase their individual fiefdoms, they become more and more untouchable. If they have to work together to accomplish their aims, they will, but only because they have to.

As harmful as those power-seeking frauds have been up to now, our government was so well set up by the Founding Fathers that up to this point in time, even their greed and dishonesty has been limited in the damage it could to our republic. That is until something happened that was unforeseen by the Founding Fathers.

The Founding Fathers evidently were well acquainted with greedy people and had a good understanding of how to set up the new government to limit the damage that dishonesty could do to us. The one thing that they didn't seem to prepare for was intentional harm to the United States from inside the government. They prepared for dishonesty, greed, and stupidity, but evidently it never occurred to them that people inside the federal government would actually work toward the destruction of the new country.

I believe that the very large problems that we are facing now are the result of the liberals themselves having their process hijacked by political insiders with a new, much more destructive agenda. Since even the liberals have not grasped the idea that anybody would continue the use of our institutions for anything beyond the personal power that the liberals crave, they either don't see or are afraid to acknowledge what is happening and are cooperating in their own demise. The very fact that they aren't actually working together on a united hidden agenda is the factor that has allowed their own, supposedly liberal policies to be hijacked and used against both the United States and the liberals who think they are still in power.

The unforeseen event that has captured the huge federal bureaucracy built for the advancement of dishonest politicians was the election of Barack Hussein Obama. Obama has taken control of everything that went before, shifted into high gear and is rapidly driving us to destruction. Naturally, he publicly uses the same justifications that the left has always used, after all, those excuses work very well. However, the difference is much more than the fact that he is doing everything on a larger scale. Unlike the machine politicians that he has captured, he does seem to have a goal other than just lining his pockets and increasing his personal power.

What Drives Obama

Okay, let's get something out of the way right up front: Barack Hussein Obama is systematically destroying the United States of America. He is running up debt that is not only unsustainable in the future—it is unsustainable now. He is using that debt to basically sell us to China as quickly as he can. I don't think that he has chosen China for any other reason than they have the money and Iran doesn't, but whatever the reason, we are being sold out.

Obama is destroying the relationships that we have with our few good allies, most notably Britain and Israel, additionally, he is bringing us closer to our enemies such as Iran and Venezuela. He is kowtowing to Russia, he plays the "race card" at every chance. So far, I have not seen any situation involving him where he hasn't turned the outcome to the detriment of the United States. In short, Barack Obama is pulling the United States apart and putting us at a disadvantage at every opportunity.

As far as I am concerned, the damage that he is doing and continues to do is a fact. Nothing more needs to be done to figure out what is happening than to simply keep up with current events. Even despite the extreme liberal bias that the media has, all the bad that Obama is doing still comes through. The fact that he is taking us down the drain so quickly that even the leftists in the media can't cover it up says a lot about the scope of the destruction.

The only real debate is why Obama is following the course that he is. To my way of thinking there are several ways to look at his actions, and I have heard many people, both private individuals and well known commentators try to explain them.

One take on the actions of Obama is that he is making all of these mistakes because he is just too inexperienced. A really good case for this point can be made by simply looking at his non-record. Checking into his background will show you that he has slipped through life and his political career by pretty much not doing anything of note and managing to not be part of any large events, either good or bad. In fact, about all his background has shown me is that he has radical friends and really likes to kill unborn, or even newly born, babies. Sadly, these traits don't make him stand out very much in a crowd of liberals.

As far as I can tell, Obama has never created a job or done any actual productive work in his life. He has never had to meet a payroll or, as it seems, even live within his actual means. But as nearly as I can determine, this is all just a smoke screen designed to elevate the vociferousness of his opposition. This type of thing—that is, his lack of any real record—inflames the right, but for the left it is just business as usual; and the liberal mind simply takes it as a matter of course. This way, he can really enrage his opponents with something that actually does damage to the left. While his liberal supporters not only don't understand that this issue is hurting them, they flat don't get what all the fuss is about, so they simply ignore it. In my opinion, Obama is only using the left to further his goals. Weakening the left while appearing to be the "underdog" the right is picking on is a very astute political move on his part that benefits him personally while keeping the few liberals that might try to resist his agenda under his thumb.

Other people believe that he makes the bad choices that he does because he is poorly advised. This thought has a lot of appeal because a quick look at the people he has appointed to key posts, maintained as friends, and retained as his advisers, will pretty much convince you that he is surrounded by a crowd that isn't going to give sage advice. There are so many radicals, mal-contents, indicted and unindicted criminals (I'm pretty sure that tax evasion is a crime, and I know that trying to blow up the pentagon is) in his circle, that if I was given guidance by Obama's group of friends and advisers, I automatically would not follow it, even if it sounded like a good idea.

There is one problem with the bad advice premise though, and that problem is that he (Obama) is the individual that selected those people. I think that if he had really wanted good advice, he would have surrounded himself with better advisers. In short, a case could be made that the reason he chose as he did was to insulate himself with people who aren't intelligent enough to get in the way of what he would really like to accomplish. Plus, they make a good smoke screen when he does something totally ridiculous like push through the health care bill or come out for cap and trade.

Both of these previous arguments assume that Obama actually intends his actions to be beneficial to the United States. This is just the old "liberals are well intentioned, just not very smart" argument but on a much larger scale. It is quite common for the average liberal citizen to defend the harmful policies of the left by saying something along the lines of "If we give this a chance, it will work." Of course, the leftist policies don't work, and when failure becomes evident to all, then the argument will become something more along the lines of "we need to modify that program, or spend more money on it." The debate between liberal and conservative on a policy will never involve the liberal saying "You're right—that didn't work, and we should get rid of that money-wasting program." The reason that this won't ever happen is because the real goal is to institute another government program that the left can then milk for money, power, and votes.

There is, however, another way of looking at what is going on in the United States and at the moment, at least at the time of this writing, the group that believes this is small, but in my experience, growing. This view is that Obama is purposefully harming our country. The thinking here is that he sought the office of the presidency for the very fact that more harm could be done to America from that office than any other place. The people who believe this also usually believe that he is a Muslim fundamentalist, and that explains why he is going to such great lengths to harm our society. This view makes a lot of sense when you factor in how badly he treats Israel. Doing things like making the Israeli prime minister cool his heels in an empty office can't possibly serve any purpose other than as a personal insult.

As I said, I know that saying Barack Hussein Obama is a Muslim and means to destroy Western civilization in general and the United States and Israel in particular is going to be viewed as a radical stand, but this is what I believe. The reason that I think this way is because I cannot swallow the idea that any well-meaning individual, criminal, or just plain vanilla crooked politician could possibly do as much accidental harm to our society as Obama has done and clearly intends to continue doing.

Even though there are a lot of different opinions about why Obama is behaving as he is, the *why* actually is not very important. What's really important is his actions. It's not going to matter all that much if he destroys our society because he is ignorant, poorly advised, a religious fanatic, or a raving megalomaniac; the extent of the damage is going to be very important, but the reason behind it won't change what happened.

I think that Obama has taken the social progressive, liberal democrat, leftist foundation that the liberals have been constructing for years, disguised himself as a radical liberal and started us on the path to ruin that he so craves. I additionally think that he has done this intentionally, but as I said whether or not he is tearing apart the United States on purpose or accidentally won't make a lot of difference in the end.

I stopped listening to what Obama says quite some time ago; instead, I concentrate on what he is actually doing. I found that even though he does say exactly what he plans to do on occasion (fundamental change comes to mind), most of the time, the improvements he claims to want for our country and the action that follows have little resemblance to each other.

Obama himself has said that he would rather be a really good one-term president than a mediocre two-term president. If you look at this phrase, this means that not only is Obama himself going to be the person who decides what the definition of *really good* is, but also he understands that the rest of us aren't going to agree with that definition. After all, if the majority of the United States thought that he was a really good president, then all he would have to do to get elected to a second term would be to not forget to run for it.

Obama points at the health care bill that he pushed through against the wishes of a majority of Americans as the pinnacle of his accomplishments. This bill, which he seems to regard as his crowning achievement, is going to ruin one of the world's best health care systems, and there is little doubt that it is going to fiscally break the United

States. For Obama to be happier about passing this bill than any other thing he has done, well, it just points out his actual goals to me.

Barack Obama would have us believe that he is working for the betterment of the United States and world society. That is what he publicly espouses, and indeed, that is what a United States president is supposed to do. In fact, when a person becomes the president, they must swear an oath to defend the Constitution. The oath is as follows:

I [name], do solemnly swear that I will faithfully execute the office of the president of the United States, and I will to the best of my ability, preserve, protect, and defend the Constitution of the United States.

This oath is short and to the point. While I understand that there can be a lot of different schools of thought on exactly what defending the Constitution means, I fail to see how what is coming out of the office of the Presidency now can be construed as any form of defense for this fundamental, founding document.

I have not personally noted anything that Obama has done to defend or strengthen the U.S. Constitution. In fact, I think that he has done quite a bit to weaken it, and I further believe that the Constitution is one of the few things that stand between him and his goal of dissolution of Western civilization. He knows this and is weakening our hold on constitutional government at every opportunity. And since the president is supposed to be one of the prime defenders of that document, he has a lot of those opportunities.

If you still think that he is a friend of the Constitution, just take a look at his judicial appointments. While the custom has generally been for past presidents to nominate people to the judiciary who have similar political leanings as the nominating president, Obama has gone way past that. His nominees are often what we used to call radicals or extremists. In my opinion he is not appointing these people because he believes that they will steer or continue the United States down the path that he ideologically thinks is correct; he is nominating these people precisely because they are radical and not only will they be lightning rods of discord while they are in office, they will also change and damage our society in ways that will weaken us.

While only time will tell what kind of justices Sonia Sotomayor and Elena Kagan turn out to be, I think that they were appointed by Obama more for their potential to polarize the United States Supreme Court than any deep thinking legal wisdom they might possess. Does anybody out there think they will rule against the health care law when it comes before them? These two were rubber-stamped through a Senate under control of the left without (shamefully) any meaningful conservative opposition.

I would like to think that these two recent Supreme Court justices will dispense considered, thoughtful rulings. However; I'm afraid that what is actually going to happen is that just as they were supported and pushed through the confirmation process by liberal lawmakers, when laws like health care for instance, that those same liberals support, come before them, our new justices will quite probably return the favor.

I think that Obama's choice of Joe Biden, as his running mate, is just another way that he gets the right person in the right place to weaken our government. How Biden managed to keep his seat in the Senate for as long as he did is a mystery to me, but nevertheless, his political longevity gives him some appearance of being an elder statesman. In my opinion, Joe Biden is actually a man who has lived to be over sixty-five years old without ever mastering enough intelligence to control his tendency for saying the wrong thing at the exactly wrong time. Is there anybody reading this who isn't aware of the huge gaffes that Joe Biden makes on a regular basis? Does anybody really believe he was the best choice Obama could have made for vice president? The fact that he often sends Biden as his emissary just strengthens my belief about Obama's true agenda.

If you think that his appointees and advisers with whom he surrounds himself aren't a complete argument for a dislike of the Constitution, how about the health care bill? Do you think that a law forcing you—and I mean you personally—to purchase health insurance is constitutional? If you do, how would you like a law that forces you to buy a General Motors automobile? After all, Obama now has effective control of GM. Speaking of that, did you like the way he took it over?

Do you regard his personal power over what used to be a public corporation as a constitutional use of the office of the presidency?

Let's take a minute and look at what I said about a law forcing you to buy a GM car. At first glance, or taken out of context, a reasonable person would look at what I said there and possibly conclude that I had gone too far and had indulged in hyperbole. Maybe so, but what if instead of starting with a law that was directed at private citizens, Obama was to get something passed that "encouraged" businesses to purchase Chevy Volts as a certain percentage of new fleet replacements? What if this "encouragement" was couched in terms of being environmentally friendly and done to reduce our dependency on oil? Still too much of a reach? Just remember that only a few short years ago if someone had written that a law was going to be passed that forced you to buy something [health insurance] whether you actually wanted it or not, the immediate, reasonable response would have been something along the lines of "This isn't Venezuela. That can't happen in the United States because it would be unconstitutional."

Since we are on the subject of constitutionality, or at least the lack of it, let's take a look at the *czars*. I personally have never cared much for our presidents having czars, but it is a system that has been with us for a long time. Some presidents make more use of czars than others, but Obama has appointed over thirty of them. A lot of these super bureaucrats don't answer to anybody but Obama. That means that there are a large number of people with broad discretionary powers doing only Obama's bidding. I don't see how that can possibly be constitutional.

Again, I don't think that he selects these czars because they share his political views. While some of the radical people he has selected for these positions may indeed share his beliefs, I still think that his main goal in appointing them is to keep things stirred up. Using the office of the presidency to run roughshod over people and institutions has the short-term effect of giving Obama more power and the long-term effect of weakening the office of the presidency through the resentment and backlash that these appointments are generating. Remember, disunity and acrimony is what he is working for. The more bickering, unnecessary partisanship, and arguing that he can generate, the better.

Even when Glenn Beck exposed one of Obama's radical nominees to the light of day, that actually worked for the hidden agenda because it caused further division between the right and left. This helps Obama in a lot of ways, but one of the more important ones is that when the Democratic Party suffers backlash from voters, he can point at this instance and others like it to blame the right. This allows him to continue his destructive actions and policies, but still be viewed as an underdog by the left.

For me, Obama has demonstrated so much disdain for things like the Pledge of Allegiance, the national anthem, and the U.S. flag that I don't even notice these character traits in him anymore. While individual private citizens are certainly within their rights to entertain these same objectionable tendencies, they should not be the beliefs of someone that has sought out the office of the presidency and then additionally sworn to defend the U.S. Constitution.

Of course he assures us that he is actually a Christian, and to prove it he points to attending a Christian church. But wait—it's Jeremiah Wright's church. That's the place where the good Reverend curses the United States and blames the United States for the world's problems. What was going on inside that building with that outrageous church leader certainly deserves exposure to the light of day, but I think that the reason Barack Hussein Obama attended and was a member of that particular church for so many years was that it was as close as he could get to listening to a radical imam without actually attending (and being seen doing it) a mosque.

Obama saying that he didn't actually know what Wright was preaching in his church is such an outrageous statement that the only way he gets a pass on it is because the average American citizen is honest and wouldn't think of lying about something like that. Because of that innate cultural honesty, we Americans tend to think that other people are being truthful with us. As for the citizens that would themselves lie about something like this and thus fully understand that Obama is being untruthful, it doesn't bother them at all that Obama sat in Wright's church, listened to and agreed with his rhetoric, and then lied to America about it.

Obama's failed appeal for the Olympic games was just one more jab at the office of the presidency. If his appearance before the Olympic committee had been successful, he would have looked like the golden boy who could fail at nothing. This would just further cement him as the new leader or messiah that the left has been looking for. Since the Olympic committee sent him packing, it just makes him look like an underdog to the left. It also weakened the office of the presidency in the eyes of the world.

Besides insulting our allies at every opportunity and getting cozy with radical and theocratic governments, Iran is being allowed to develop nuclear weapons on Obama's watch. I think even someone as ineffectual as Jimmy Carter would at least try to prevent that from happening. Yet Barack Hussein Obama seems to be standing idly by while one of the world's most radical Islamic theocracies develops nuclear capabilities. Hello? Am I the only one who draws a conclusion from this?

From Progressivism to Destruction

While I've laid out a lot of things that I think Obama is up to, and I certainly haven't been shy about stating what I think his beliefs are and where his ultimate goals lay, even Obama could not accomplish all that he has or realistically even have been elected without a lot of groundwork being done prior to his meteoric rise.

The crazy thing about this is that the liberals and so-called social progressives have changed and shaped our government and institutions so well for Obama's purposes that he is able to step in, co-opt them, and bend things to his uses while making it seem as if he is merely carrying on their programs, just with a little more oomph than usual. I don't however think that all of what we are going through is part of any "master plan" simply because such a plan would have to have existed since about the time of World War I, and involve so many people and unforeseeable events that it just wouldn't be possible.

You're not going to find me giving liberals and so-called social progressives much credit for anything, but I will say that I don't think the damage these idiots have done to the United States was intended to culminate in someone like Obama coming to the fore and using their years of degradation as a weapon to bludgeon us into the stone age. I do think the collective effect of their years of self aggrandizing abuse has resulted in the problems that we have now and while they didn't intentionally cause our potential destruction, they didn't worry about it happening or do anything to stop it either.

Whether intentional or not, the present situation couldn't have happened without them and they obviously didn't worry about the results of their failed policies and abuses. When the liberals wake up to what they have brought down on us, their concern won't be the damage they've done, instead they will be unhappy that their reign has ended. The manner of that end and what it has done to the United States will not be important to them—all they will (and do care about) is retaining or regaining power.

As I said, I don't think that the goal of what the liberals have been doing for the last eighty years or so has been to bring Barack Obama or somebody like him to the pinnacle of power so that he can reverse a couple of centuries of progress. But I do think that the left has collectively done extensive harm to our society and our country, and there is no doubt in my mind that the harmful things they have accomplished were not done accidentally. If you spend some time thinking about the scope and breadth of the abuses and damage done to this republic by the left, it becomes hard to believe that all of it could be accidental.

With almost everything that the liberals do resulting in some kind of reduction or general deterioration of the human condition, if this weren't the general plan, then the laws of probability would kick in and some of their programs would actually be beneficial. Since they aren't, and even when policies fail so badly that the failure is evident to all thinking people, the left still backs them; I have to assume that this cumulative harm is intentional. This is why Obama has been able to use the left and their programs so effectively. Even the left can see that his ideas and programs are harmful, but to them, it just seems to be business as usual albeit on a larger scale. Either that, or they are afraid to say anything because it would mean admitting that their programs have been a failure. We'll know the democrats have decided to fess up when the party leadership goes to the White House and asks Obama to resign. Since I don't think that's going to happen, it will still be up to conservatives to get control of the situation.

In the United States, we have been subjected to a gradual eroding of our lifestyle and freedoms. The first amendment is under assault every day. The left is furious that conservative talk radio is popular and well listened to. Of course the largest attacks on free speech come from the left, and the one justification that they use is that other points of view should get equal time. So theoretically, if you had an hour of say, Rush Limbaugh, then you would have to balance it out with an hour of some liberal like Jessie Jackson, or Michael Moore. Man, that would be rough, can you imagine listening to Michael Moore for an hour? Talk about suicide rates going up. I would find myself in the unusual position of wishing for the commercial break.

Even though free speech is article one in the Bill of Rights, and the left is all for it when it supposedly calls for burning the Stars and Stripes; when this same free speech involves talking about failed liberal policies or things that the left doesn't like—then, according to the left, it needs some regulation in the name of "fairness." Guess who gets to decide what's fair? If you said the left, you are correct. Conservatives find some of the things that constitute free speech disgusting, but seldom do you hear a conservative trying to gain control of the First Amendment. If you were to hear one speak out against free speech, they would quickly be disowned by the rest.

Since the leftists hate the capitalist system so badly (you know, the system that rewards good ideas and hard labor), they just can't understand why talk radio is so conservative. They cannot grasp the idea that people listen to what they like and agree with. They can, however understand that this conservative platform makes it harder for them to run roughshod over the general population, so while they can't figure it out, they understandably want to silence it.

An excellent example of how badly the left misunderstands talk radio, and how much they are frustrated by it is the failed Air America network. Giving their best and brightest a spot on the airwaves failed both spectacularly and publicly. I was doing some traveling during this (short) time period when Air America existed, and I listened to it when I could. Since truth and facts don't fit well with the liberal agenda, I was curious what they would talk about. Basically, all of it that I heard had two main central themes. These subjects were one, conservatives are bad, and two, Rush Limbaugh is worse. That was pretty much all I took from their discussions, and while it was amusing, it was a little short on any real substance. It would have been hilarious to me, except for the sad fact that those types of people have real power in this country.

The left argues that a lot of the conservative free speech is hate speech and untrue. President Clinton even blamed the Oklahoma City bombing on talk radio. The left is constantly accusing the people on the right of "going too far" and abusing the First Amendment. The left, and their liberal handmaiden, the press, hold conservatives to a pretty high standard where free speech is concerned. On the other hand, the left can say nearly anything vile and despicable that they like, and as far as I can tell, they will get a free pass from the press.

One example of the double standard concerning free speech is when Trent Lott was all but run out of town on a rail for merely paying Strom Thurmond an offhand compliment at Thurmond's retirement party. Just saying something nice to a retiring politician at a private party caused such uproar that Lott had to resign his leadership position in the Senate. I can't remember hearing any such ruckus after Robert (former kleagle for the ku klux klan) Byrd used the word @#*%!@ (sorry, I'm just not going to print that) twice on national television.

If liberals insist on putting limits on free speech, how about one that deals with being truthful? Don't get me wrong, I firmly believe that the First Amendment is one of the biggest things between us and a dictatorship. I don't want limits on free speech, and as distasteful as some of the things that result from unbridled free speech are, putting up with free speech that we don't like is nothing in comparison to what would happen to us if free speech was restricted. I just think if you scared the liberals with the thought that they would lose the ability to tell bald-faced lies whenever and wherever they like, we would have a lot more peace and quiet in this country.

Hey, I have an idea; the left is always trying to dust off the fairness doctrine that I mentioned, so how about we change the fairness doctrine from even amounts of airtime to even amounts of truth. Every time a conservative tells the truth, you know, something like the federal government spends too much money, a liberal would then have to say something true from their side. They could respond to our hypothetical conservative with something like the war on poverty is worki…. Well, that wouldn't work. How about, when we take in extra tax revenue it goes to paying off the national de….. Hmmm, can't use that one either. Okay, they could say, the Department of Energy is decreasing our dependence on foreign oi…Oh. I know, I did not have sex with that wom…Shoot. I guess we can see why the liberals are pretty sparing in their use of the truth and facts instead of rhetoric, repetition, and volume.

Actually, when I see conservatives and liberals debating, it usually isn't long before the facts on the conservative side will disturb the leftist, and a personal attack will ensue. Liberals use lots of tactics to overcome a lack of truth and knowledge. Some but not all of these tricks are emotional outbursts, talking over other people, refusing to answer for various reasons, changing the subject, etc., and finally, (this is not original with me), you can really tell when a liberal has totally lost the argument when they start unjustly comparing conservatives to a nazi or Hitler. Something that I draw a great deal of amusement from is the fact that relating an action of any liberal to that of a nazi or Hitler will draw the wrath of a majority of the left, and additionally, the main stream media. At almost any given hour of the day, some liberal somewhere is publicly using the term nazi to denigrate a conservative, yet let one conservative do the same thing, justly or unjustly, and the left and the press will just go off.

What the leftists have created is an environment that is poisoned with their constant rhetoric against the right and against our basic institutions such as Christianity, the traditional family, a solid work ethic, and any number of other things that are the foundations of our society. The reason that they have done this is to forward their policy of government control and intervention in our lives.

The single goal of all the true leftists is power, money, and power over money. The disguise they use for this attack on things that are so important to our society is social progressiveness. Even when they are making someone take down a nativity scene or a copy of the Ten Commandments, they will claim to be doing it for the good of society. A crucifix in a jar of urine, they claim, is art. And not just any art, but government-funded art. Not only that, but I bet that the expression of that art is protected free speech. The conservative reaction to this distasteful display was not to attack free speech, but to attempt to de-fund the federal program that paid for that particular piece of "art". The liberal reaction to Rush Limbaugh and other conservative talk radio hosts is to try and reinstate the fairness doctrine so they can eliminate free speech for conservative talk show hosts.

This has been done with the complicity of our so-called "mainstream media," which even bends over so far as to aid the liberals in their attacks on free speech. The liberal bias of a large portion of our media is so obvious that the most astonishing thing about it is that the media denies the existence of any bias.

What the leftists have intentionally done is create an environment where they can push their programs, control large portions of our society, keep the general citizenry in line, and foster more spending and more government. This they have done on purpose. No matter what they might say publicly, if you watch what they do instead of listen to what they say, the result of their actions is the ballooning of government, spending, and the increase in their power and wealth that goes with it.

What they have unintentionally created is an environment where somebody like Obama can come in and take the abuses that have been done, and turn all of that to his personal goals. I have already stated my opinion about where Obama wants to take us, and believe me it will definitely be the fundamental change that he mentioned when he was campaigning.

Regardless of Obama's actual beliefs and where he thinks he is going, the fact remains that he has captured the bloated federal government and the liberal machine that created it and is using that bureaucracy to tear our society apart. The real irony here is that he is destroying the Democratic Party as fast as or faster than he is tearing the country apart.

On purpose or not, the progressives have over legislated, overspent, and corrupted the process of the federal government until instead of a government of the people, by the people, and for the people, we now have a bloated, corrupt, intrusive, big-spending bureaucracy that is the antithesis of what our founding fathers envisioned. This government has come under the control of Barack Obama who, intentionally or not, is increasing and hastening the destructive programs of the left.

The Coming Struggle Is Here

The leftists would like you to think that the present struggle between liberals and conservatives is a simple argument to try and determine the philosophical direction that the United States is going to head for the next few years. A mere debate if you would, between two groups of well-intentioned people over which one is going to lead us into the future, and how that future will be shaped. They would have you believe that no matter how it works out, the basic fabric of our society will be unchanged and, indeed, if the liberals "win," we will be a kinder, gentler, more-respected, better-led, and happier society.

At the time of this writing, the leftists are at a little bit of a political disadvantage. If the new conservatives in the house, combined with the few actual conservatives that were already there, continue on the course they have promised, they are going to cause problems for the liberals. On top of that, if the conservatives do as they said they will, then not only are the liberals going to have problems with them, it is very likely that the taxpayers are going to notice some actual progress made in our federal government and encourage that by electing more conservatives in the 2012 elections.

It is way too soon to do anything other than dream of how the next round of elections might go, but if the citizens of our great country approach the polls then in the same state of mind that they did in 2010, then it probably isn't going to work out well for the bureaucrats and power seekers.

As I've mentioned, I'm no political guru, and if I can figure that out, you bet the leftists in power have pictured it also. That's why they are out there right now preaching "bipartisanship" and "reaching across the aisle."

There are two main points that I would like to make about bi-partisanship. One, the left only uses this term when they are trying to get conservatives to do something that is against conservative values. This is a case where they basically use the values of the right, in this instance the spirit of cooperation and fair play, to get the conservatives to cooperate in doing something that is against those same values. Sound silly? If it wasn't against the values of the right, then conservatives would already be on board with it, and there wouldn't be any need for cooperation in the spirit of bipartisanship. So when you hear the left preaching bipartisanship, it's a safe bet that they are trying to accomplish something that shouldn't be done.

Second, and to my mind the most important is that if voters have elected conservatives and sent them to congress with a clear message that they are expecting conservative action in the federal government, then *reaching across the aisle* isn't what these congressman are supposed to be doing.

With the state of affairs that exist in this country right now, it is time for the politicians that have previously supported the left to practice this theoretical bipartisanship. The ones that actually care about the country can start working with conservatives on salvaging this mess that is the federal government. The ones that are only interested in increasing their power over people and money can make themselves known by fighting to maintain the status quo.

Let's find out who are the actual ideologues that really do believe in the United States and who are really unindicted co-conspirators in the ruination of our republic. Let's put the failing policies of the left up to open, recorded votes and see where all of our politicians stand. Now isn't the time for bipartisanship; now is the time to step forward, vote, and stand behind those votes.

What the liberals want us to believe is that they are the kinder and gentler politicians, who would like nothing better than for their more unruly, slightly less refined conservative colleagues to "reach across the aisle" so that the federal government can continue governing for the betterment of all people. At every opportunity they preach the gibberish that is supposed to convince the electorate that as liberals they are wiser, elder statesman. The liberals are very good at spouting nonsense so publicly and so often that they actually convince people that the leftist, power-seeking policies they push so hard are actually beneficial. I for one would not want to be the person who has to go out and explain how *cap and tax* is going to be a good program. Yet the liberals have people out there every day touting their elitist, socialist, entitlement programs, and doing it convincingly. Talk about marketers, these people can sell anything.

Just to put a point on it, during the lame duck session of the 2010 Congress, Nancy Pelosi was very publicly telling the citizens of this country that we must extend the unemployment insurance beyond two years because paying out this insurance creates jobs. It may be that they put Pelosi out front on this issue because she was the only person that could say something like that with a straight face, but just the fact that they were willing to put a statement so idiotic on the airwaves tells you a lot about how liberals think and operate. Actually, constantly extending the unemployment compensation period does have an effect on jobs, just not the effect that they are telling you about. Government bureaucratic jobs are created or maintained, and private sector job creation is stifled because of the cost of the program, and the fact that people are basically being paid to not work, so there is a lot less incentive to get out and "do something". That something they aren't doing being work or starting their own business. Stop paying so much unemployment and you will start seeing more people getting serious about finding something to do.

If Ms. Pelosi really truly believes that paying unemployed people through the unemployment program actually creates jobs, then why doesn't she carry that thought to its logical conclusion and suggest that we send these very same job creators (as per Pelosi's public statements) four times the money that we are sending them now. Wouldn't that create four times the jobs they are presently creating and everybody could just go back to work? I really can see only two reasons the liberals haven't suggested something like this. The first being that even they realize that what they have already said is so idiotic that it just can't be taken any further, or they just haven't thought of it yet. Since one litmus test that the left doesn't seem to use before they speak is whether what they are saying is true or even logical, maybe one of these days Mrs. Pelosi will indeed come out for increasing the amount of unemployment checks to create more jobs. After all, she shoved the health care bill through the house by using bribery and threats, and then told the entire world what a good thing it was. After that, an idiotic statement about unemployment benefits is not going to be the dumbest thing she ever said.

Despite what the liberal powerbrokers want you to think, what is going on in the United States right now is not some minor spat over inconsequential idealistic differences. What is really going on is a struggle to determine the fate of the United States of America.

On one side we have the liberals that want to continue down the path of financial and moral irresponsibility and corruption. This group is led by Barack Hussein Obama, who has co-opted the radical liberal movement for his own purposes, whatever they are. Even without the extra influence of Obama, if we are to continue with the old liberal power policies, we have reached the point of no return. The United States will no longer be able to sustain the taxation, spending, and borrowing policies of the left. These policies aren't something that we *should* change; they are something that we *must* change. "Things" aren't about to get serious; they are serious now.

If we don't make a major, fundamental shift in the way the federal government spends money and stop it from invading and controlling the day-to-day activities of our citizens, then what we know as the United States of America will eventually (probably sooner than later) cease to exist as we know it. There likely will continue to be a country called the United State of America, but it will only bear passing resemblance to the great country that we now call the United States.

The leftists, or liberals, or social progressives, or however you would prefer to label them (and I'm not the first person to print this, but it is correct) that have seized power in the United States don't just have a different political way of thinking, they are the enemy. These people have been and are heading us down the path of big spending, bigger borrowing, and intrusive, freedom-stealing federal government. Even the fact that Obama has taken that to the "next level" only means that we lost the opportunity to deal with it later and must make changes now.

While Obama obviously doesn't care for capitalism and Western civilization, he doesn't understand them, and if anything is going to save us from him, that lack of understanding will be it. He is basically devoting his life and career to dismantling something (Western civilization and the American work ethic) while not building or creating anything. Our Christian foundation, and capitalist society are forces for human improvement that he just can't comprehend. However, whether he understands these principles or not, he and the left do know that in order to be successful in their aims, they need to keep us from returning to these ideals.

While the left is trying to convince America that this mere argument between friendly but slightly dissimilar philosophies is a minor debate, and there is no reason for heated rhetoric or uncivil behavior, they are out there preaching their usual divisive rhetoric. Mere days after the tragic shooting in Arizona, Representative Steve Cohen, a Democrat from Tennessee, was comparing Republican statements about health care to nazi propaganda; and on the floor of the U.S. House of Representatives I might add. It doesn't seem to me that the supposed party of tolerance is very tolerant. The leftists resort to calling opponents *nazi* and *Hitler* so much that the real surprise about Mr. Cohen's use of such terms is that it didn't come sooner. I could have called that one, oh wait, I did.

The most amusing thing about what he said, besides its predictability, is the fact that after he was called out on it, he said that he wasn't actually comparing Republicans to nazis. I don't know, it looks to me like he was, but if there are any authorities on comparing people to nazis and Hitler, it is the left of which he is a member, so he certainly knows more about the rules involved with calling people nazis than I do.

Anyway, while the left is speaking to their opponents and United States citizens about cooperation and civility, at the same time there is no rule they won't bend, no law they won't break, no name calling to which they won't resort, no rhetoric that is too inflammatory, and worst of all, no rights they won't trample in pursuit of their goals.

If you think Obama and the left aren't willing to sacrifice your rights, hold your breath until Eric Holder (United States attorney general) finally prosecutes the new black panthers for voter intimidation.

Part of the reason that the leftists do all of this is because to get the public to go along with them, they have to convince a majority of the voters that this is just the way things are, and even though we wish it could "be better", the world is just a place of gray issues, and we must muddle through without achieving lofty goals. This is of course not true, but by constantly bombarding us with propaganda that tells us how limited we are, the liberals are able to spread discouragement and malaise. Remember the goal of the leftists is maintaining the status quo, and they regard the best possible outcome to be a continual growth of government bureaucracies and power.

While the liberals are constantly trying to paint the world as a dull shade of gray with no black and white issues, if you notice, when it comes to some of the things that they want to argue, like the death penalty, they will refer to that as an issue that is black and white. In the death penalty debate, they say a lot of things against the death penalty, but one argument that they always use is that innocent people get convicted and put to death. That's a pretty black and white statement if you ask me. Another thing they say about the death penalty is that it isn't a deterrent. Now, that's just not true. I defy anybody to name one criminal that has suffered the death penalty that went on to commit another crime. With a zero recidivism rate, the death penalty seems to be a fairly effective deterrent, but I digress.

Sadly, as much use as Obama makes of the tactics described above, none of them are original with him. Whatever Obama's actual goals are and wherever his true sympathies lie, the biggest difference between him and the leftist power seekers that have preceded him is the scale of the damage and how much more adept he is than those that have gone before him. I don't know if he is such an effective manipulator because he is just that much smarter than the other liberals or if he is so superior at political exploitation because he has a goal beyond maintaining the normal status quo.

Obama and the left are out there fighting everyday for their goals (whatever they are). It is past time for American citizens to realize that we are in a struggle not only for our republic, but our children's future. It's not only time to wake up, it's time to get involved and defeat the liberal socialists and Obama in the arena of ideas and more importantly, implementation of those ideas.

Definition of a Taxpayer

Since I am one, I thought the term *taxpayer* could use some clarity. The term taxpayer is getting a lot of ink these days, but that really is nothing new. Ever since the liberal dismantling of our society began, it has been very important to the left that they redefine this term and cloud people's understanding of exactly what a taxpayer is, and more importantly how they fit into our capitalist society.

Actually, if you wanted to boil it down to the nuts and bolts, at least for the discussion about government revenues, it would be simple to just say there are two groups. Most people would simply call those two groups the haves, and the have nots. I disagree; there are a lot of hard working people out there that are doing their level best to hold their heads above water and be successful. Some of them will make it, and some will not, but while they are struggling, they are paying taxes (part of why they are struggling). If you were to interview some of the people in this position, I doubt that they would class themselves as *haves*. I think they would probably class themselves as *hope to haves*.

In my opinion, a much clearer definition would be net revenue producers (aka taxpayers) and revenue consumers. That's a pretty easy definition to make: if you pay more taxes during the year than you get back at tax-refund time or receive as some kind of government assistance, congratulations—you are a taxpayer. The second group is even easier to identify; if you aren't a taxpayer (revenue producer), you are a revenue consumer.

The second group (consumers) has a subset, the drones in our federal government, the useless bureaucrats. Unfortunately, government cannot run itself, but we have way more federal programs and federal employees than are actually necessary, a lot more.

If you talk to one of these superfluous federal employees, that is if you absolutely can't get out of it, they would be adamant about the fact that they are indeed taxpayers because income taxes are taken from them on payday just like everybody else.

Some of the huge bureaucracy that I continually rail against really is necessary. The military (which the liberals hate) is so important that we literally wouldn't be here without it. Although they have a lot of extra people, the FAA is pretty important. The FDA is a hugely bloated and inefficient organization, but some of what they do is indispensible.

Even though some of the government employees are necessary, they still are net users of tax revenue. The fed may be taking taxes from them, but they still depend on the federal government for that paycheck.

Let me pause here and be very clear about something, paid from federal revenues or not, military personnel are largely underpaid. If we had less of the useless type of federal employees, then we could treat our service people better. Liberals constantly say that the conservatives want to pay the military better and keep taxes low at the same time. They say this as if it is a pejorative, and then they add that it isn't possible. They are half right; conservatives do advocate better funding for the military and not raising taxes to do it. Actually, being half right is pretty good for a liberal, it's a lot closer than they usually get. The half that they get wrong is asserting that we can't keep taxes low and pay the service people better. Of course we can. This is just more of the liberals trying to tell us that instead of a spending problem we have a revenue problem. I bet if we cut the Department of Education's budget in half, we could have more money for the military with no change in tax rates. Hey, that would be a real win-win because we could probably improve education if we could get the fed out of the schools. I bet we could spare a bunch of Department of Energy employees, too.

If you can't figure out which are the necessary federal employees and which aren't, try to think of the ones that if they didn't come back to work or if one day just up and quit, they wouldn't actually leave a vacancy. You know like the previously mentioned department of education, or any government employee that is involved with climate change, probably half of the state department and so on. Another good test would be if a trained monkey could do the job better, then we probably don't need a federal employee for it (think TSA).

Taxpayers are really not that hard to recognize, one location where you can find a lot of taxpayers is at a place called work. For a person to have to pay income tax, or capital gains tax, they have to have earned something, or received some income or payments of some type. Most taxpayers deal with the income tax as something that is deducted from the pay that they receive for performing some kind of job.

What's really important about the fact that income tax is levied as a percentage of gross wage receipts is the fact that the more money a person receives as compensation for their time and labor, the more revenue the government gets as tax money. You would think that pretty quickly the bureaucrats would figure out that if they want a lot of money to spend so their personal fiefdoms could be held and grown, that they need to encourage productivity. After all, more production would mean more people making money and that means more income tax collected and deposited in government coffers. Unfortunately, subtracting people from the category of revenue consumers and turning them into productive taxpayers, works out badly for bureaucrats.

Revenue consumers as a group are notoriously unconcerned about where the money to pay for the programs they are using comes from. In fact there are a lot of them that feel they are *entitled* to benefits and as long as the free housing, welfare checks, subsidized transportation, free food, free medical care, etc. is available and uninterrupted, they are good with the status quo. How much their government benefits cost or where the money is coming from to pay for them isn't something they worry over very much. In fact, many of the beneficiaries of these programs think they are *owed* their entitlement status and will be very vocal about the fact that what it costs taxpayers doesn't matter because it is their right to receive benefits.

On the other hand taxpayers look at the amount of money deducted from their paychecks, and become very concerned with how all of the government programs are being financed. For the liberal agenda to succeed, they need as many people to be revenue consumers as they can get. A big majority of taxpayers versus tax consumers is not going to work out well for bureaucrats whose jobs depend on doling out large amounts of government largesse.

Taxpayers are much less likely to feel that some faceless group of people is entitled to receive hard-earned money taken from paychecks. In fact, given enough reason, they will get together and make these feelings known at the federal level. As this is a threat to the leftists, they try to avoid the circumstances that might cause this to happen.

The ways that the left gets around taxpayers concerns to continue handing out money are numerous. The liberals are very, very clever at maintaining and expanding their power base.   One of the more obvious ways that they get by with what they do to the average taxpayer is by continually borrowing. There is no question that conservative and liberal politicians have both contributed to this sorry state of affairs that has become our national debt (and our national shame), but the liberals are using, and always have used, the funds they garner in this way as more money to further control our society.

With borrowed money, in the short term they can deduct less from the taxpayers' paycheck and therefore keep the taxpayers somewhat complacent. Long term, they have to increase the amount they take away from the producers to pay the interest on the debt while continuing and increasing federal programs. You would think that when they eventually have to confiscate more money because of the interest on the debt, the taxpayers would get wise and say something about the big percentage of income that the fed is skimming out of their paychecks. This is where the liberals show some of their extreme marketing skills. When approached by actual taxpayers about this issue, instead of owning up to the problem and admitting that we are overspending, they say that they would rather not take so much money, but that the extra revenue must be collected to pay down the national debt.

In one fell swoop, they frame the amount of money that they are wasting as a revenue problem, blame it on the people that came before them, color themselves as righteous individuals that just want to pay the debt back, imply that taxpayers should cough up the dough for the good of the country, and this is the most important part; draw attention away from the fact that too much money is being spent. The kicker is that if they do get extra revenue, it won't be used to pay down the national debt. Historically, extra revenue just gets spent. Liberals are probably some of the best marketers the world has ever known. Couple their marketing skills with the cooperation they get from the media, and taxpayers hardly have a chance. Of course leftists have had a lot of practice, and they are tenacious beyond belief.

As much money as your average liberal can borrow and spend, they are still small time compared to Barack Hussein Obama. He has taken this borrowing to new, unprecedented heights. Since the interest on the debt and the size of that debt will stifle our economy, directly affect our quality of life, and negatively impact our society as a whole, he is of course, all for borrowing as much money as possible and even worse, putting in place new entitlement programs that will turn into ongoing money pits of previously unknown proportions.

For the most part, taxpayers are people who are working, producing, and doing things. These are the people who move the United States along from day to day. They are the utility employee that keeps the electricity flowing, the plumber that takes care of your plumbing problems, the airline pilot that gets you safely to your destination, the convenience store cashier that sells you coffee, and on and on and on. These people (probably you, too) are what makes everything work and most of them share one quality. From the lowliest ditch digger (by the way, I have dug ditches for a living) to the highest paid corporate executive (unfortunately, that's a job I haven't held), they are almost all busy. They have work to do, need to get it done, and would like to get whatever they are working on finished so they can go to whatever is next.

What busy people don't want to make time for is dealing with problems that somebody else has created and dumped on them. That's one of the ways that the liberal agenda has gone as far as it has even though a lot of working people (taxpayers) disagree with some or all of it. Ask most taxpayers what they think of pork-barrel spending, and you will usually get a pretty straight forward response against it.

As much as taxpayers dislike how the government milks them, very few busy people want to take on the burden of becoming politically active, organizing, and doing something about it. Liberals know this and that is why most of the money-wasting programs that they so like to administrate are usually grown slowly over years.

Since actual, politically aware taxpayers are usually against liberal policies, a lot of the federal programs are designed to make these taxpayers partially or wholly dependent on government programs. If, in spite of leftists' best efforts, somebody just insists on making their own way through life by being a working, contributing member of society and refuses to become a ward of some federal entitlement, then they may have to be coerced in some other way.

I happen to live near a large military base, the threat of this base being closed and the resulting economic loss to the town I and about one hundred thousand other people live in has been brought up several times. Don't think that this kind of strategy is either rare or ineffective.

As I keep harping on, liberals are very clever at getting their way and convincing the public to go along with them even when it clearly is not in society's best interest. An argument against funding cuts that leftists like to trot out whenever necessary is that they will have to cut services. Of course cuts in revenue will mean reduced services; it doesn't take a rocket scientist to figure that one out. I personally, am willing to sacrifice and do without the Department of Education, the Department of Energy, the TSA, and all of Obama's czars. I know, that sounds like a real hardship, but I'm willing to give it a shot.

The way the liberals frame this fact to be an argument in their favor is to be very selective in what services are going to be cut. As soon as a possible reduction in budget is perceived, they start talking about reducing the number of policeman, fire fighters, teachers, and discussing the cuts they are going to make to the military. It seems that any and all budget cuts must be met by getting rid of the most important, useful people first. If it were left up to me, I would start by getting rid of useless bureaucrats. I bet we can eliminate a whole bunch of them before we get to any fire fighters or police.

Just the thought of how many bureaucrats we can put out into the real working world brings a big smile to my face. You know the real working world—the one where you have to be on time, on budget, attentive, and polite to customers. Just imagine the TSA agent who was molesting you last week could be asking you if you would like fries with that. Sorry, I was daydreaming again. Where were we?

If a parks department budget is threatened, then the first thing they would have to do is close the Washington Monument. Is the Washington Monument really the place the parks department would have to begin cutting if they had their budget reduced? Surely we have some smaller, slightly less important public park that could be downsized or closed. This type of defense against budget cuts would be laughable, except it seems to work. Now that's definitely not funny.

The American taxpayer is the foundation of our economic system. Whether the left likes it or not, the people who participate in the capitalist system by working and being productive are who have financed this nation from the very beginning. When the left finally saps enough of the work ethic out of our workforce, either by soul-sucking social-equality programs or by confiscating so much income that people can no longer justify going to work, our working citizens will stop producing. When that happens, our economic system will collapse.

The other side of that same coin is that if we could get rid of some of these social programs that are so detrimental to the human condition and our country, we could increase the workforce (add taxpayers), reduce government expenditures, and (this is really important) give the existing working class a big morale boost.

If we want to improve our economy, and who doesn't, how about we take this opportunity to give the people that actually carry that economy (taxpayers) on their shoulders a helping hand. Instead of confiscating more of their money, let's just start using the money that is taken as taxes more wisely.

Assaulting Taxpayers with Tax Dollars

The federal government often controls state governments by withholding *federal money* from states if the states don't comply with the federal government's rules or if they want the state government to do something that a particular state or several states are resisting. Good examples of this are the old fifty-five-mile-per-hour speed limit, and the twenty-one-year-old drinking age.

In the case of the fifty five mile per hour speed limit, since the federal government does not have the authority to set a national speed limit, what they did was threaten to withhold federal highway matching funds from states that didn't set their highway speed limits at fifty five or lower. It took some time and some other arm twisting, but the feds eventually got the national fifty-five-mile-per-hour speed limit that was supposed to save us.

I don't recall exactly how the feds twisted the arms of states that resisted the twenty-one-year-old drinking limit, but I'm sure it also involved withholding some kind of funding. I do agree with the twenty-one-year-old drinking age, but I don't think that it is any business of the federal government. What the legal drinking age is, or for that matter how fast we drive, in a particular state should be a matter between the state government and the citizens of that state, not what the feds tells the state it should be.

Another way that the national government exercises control over states in areas where legally, they have little or no authority is by furnishing money for projects. When they do this, the funding comes with all kinds of strings attached. The attitude of the federal government seems to be that since they are paying for it, they should be able to dictate any details of the project that they would like. The effect of this "since we're paying for it, you have to do it like we want" attitude is a win win for the feds on several different levels.

First, on the surface of it, it does seem reasonable to follow the wishes of the entity paying for the work. After all, if you hired someone to build a house for you and they built something different than you wanted, not only would you withhold any monies they wanted, there is a good chance that you would take them to court. So an example like I just gave would make it seem that in this instance, the fed is correct in their attitude and since they are indeed paying the bill, they should get what they want. After all, the state or other municipality always has the option of not having to comply with attached rules and regulations by just refusing the money, or at least that's how it would appear.

Comparing the house builder above and the process the federal government uses may seem reasonable on the surface, but there is a very large difference between the two situations. A person or company that hires another entity to do work, buys a product, or enters into any financial agreement uses their own money or at least money that they will be ultimately responsible for. The heart of our capitalist system is people exchanging money that they have with other people for goods or services. So the above home builder is seeking something he doesn't have or desires more of (money in this case) from somebody who has it but needs the services that the builder supplies.

This is all pretty straight forward, and the only difference between buying a house from a home builder and getting a soft drink at the convenience store is one of scale. In both cases, money is being exchanged between two parties for goods and/or services. These are just examples of capitalism at work that happen billions of times a day, every day. In effect, it's business as usual.

However, when the federal government spends money, it is not business as usual. When the government does business, they are not participating in the capitalist system because the government is not using money that it has earned or created by profitable enterprise. The money the government spends is revenue that it has received from taxes it confiscates from citizens or fees that it charges for certain services (fees are actually taxes by another name). The federal government has no other source of income besides taxes. While some taxation is necessary, all taxes, necessary or not, are money that has been taken from somebody or from some kind of entity (such as corporations, foundations, or some other kind of legal entity). Since all other entities are made up of people or groups of people, like investors, members, or owners, taxes ultimately are all paid by individuals. By the way, the purpose of taxes is NOT as Obama said to "spread the wealth around." That is indeed the liberal agenda, except he left out the part where as much as possible is supposed to stick to the liberals that decide who does and doesn't get this largesse.

Anyway, back to what is really happening when the federal government does business. We have already established that when the federal government buys any kind of goods or services, basically if they do any kind of business at all, it is always with money that they have taken in some form or other from taxpayers. By the way, even if it is borrowed money or money that the Federal Reserve just decided to print, ultimately, the taxpayer is on the hook for it in one way or another. The federal government cannot spend any other kind of money besides taxpayer money because when you are talking about the government, no other kind exists. So the next time a liberal politician tries to tell you that funding something is not going to cost anything, that politician is flat out lying, no exceptions.

So if we apply the example of the homebuilding contractor to the federal government telling states how the federal (taxpayer) dollars should be utilized, we have to make some changes to the transaction. Now the state is being told to use money that the federal government confiscated from the state's own citizens in the manner that the feds wants it spent. If the state refuses, then they (the feds) just withhold the money. It's as if the homebuyer took money away from the home builder, hired the home builder using the same money that was taken away (confiscated) from the builder, and then told the poor home builder, "If you don't get it exactly like I want it, I won't let you have your money back." Now what is going on is a lot more like the home builder paying for and constructing the house, but having to do it to the very exacting standards of the person that took his money to start with. That isn't just confusing, it's not right, but it happens all the time between the federal government and our other governing bodies. If it seems to you that trying to follow this particular money trail is confusing, remember that it is confusing on purpose. Fiscal clarity in circumstances like this works against the left, so they make it as convoluted and unclear as possible. Think about it, when the government threatens to withhold federal dollars that sounds a lot different than "We won't give you your money back," but it is exactly the same thing.

So when the federal government tells states that they (the fed) will fund, or help fund, a project, but only if it is done under ultimate federal control so that they can be sure the federal standards are followed, that states taxpayers are being forced to do something in a certain manner by the threat of withholding the very tax dollars that these same citizens have already paid expressly to fund the very services the federal government is threatening to withhold. If a private or corporate entity did something like that, it would be fraud, and I imagine that it would also be prosecutable.

When the federal government threatens to withhold money (tax dollars) until a state takes a certain action, like changing the speed limit, or enacting a certain law, I think that bears a real resemblance to extortion, and I know that's prosecutable in the private sector.

I have heard a few whispers of the new conservatives elected to the 2011 Congress suggesting that federal funds be withheld from the so-called sanctuary cities like San Francisco. While I think it would be hilarious to turn the liberals' own methods of taxpayer abuse on them, I am dead set against taxpayer exploitation, and I hope that we don't go down this road. There are plenty of methods existing in the criminal law already to deal with these lawbreakers without resorting to something as disgusting as using taxpayers money against taxpayers. Surely anybody in a position to enforce the law who chooses not to is committing a crime and should be prosecuted to the full extent of the law. As amusing as it would be to turn the tables on the leftists in this manner, we already have enough politicians that behave unethically, and we don't need any more of this kind of behavior.

As bad of a usurpation and dilution of the authority of states governments that everything we've discussed up to this point is, the federal government has a much better way of undercutting state authorities and the taxpayers that make up a state. The most effective way that the feds have of emasculating state governments is by dealing directly with municipal entities. It's going to be very difficult for a state government to work up the backbone to take the federal government on and say enough is enough, when the federal government is already dealing directly with nearly every county (or parish), city, and school district that exists in that state.

All the techniques that we have already covered that the federal government uses to deal with the states they also use on the smaller municipal governments. If a state government can't stand up by itself to the power-sucking, money-grabbing monster called the federal government, then how well is a small town going to do trying to fight the same battle? The answer is that the feds are going to crush any municipal government that tries to stand up to them.

So why does the federal government do all of this? If you could actually pin a liberal talking head down, I think the answer would be something misleading and/or nonsensical along the lines of having to maintain standards or equality across all fifty states (not fifty seven as Obama once said) and that the only way for things to be uniform and compatible throughout the nation is for the federal government to be in charge and be the ultimate regulating authority. Whatever the answer is, it most likely will be something about the federal government having to do the things that it does for the national good.

I think the real reason that the federal government allocates, or doesn't allocate, funds is for control. The more control the federal government can take from smaller governments that are subject to local residents, the better for the liberal agenda.

By renaming tax revenue *federal dollars,* the national government has developed a powerful weapon that can be used as a carrot or a stick, depending on the situation. What they have done is turned our own tax dollars, furnished by us as taxpayers, into the crack cocaine of the government world. By use of past and present liberal spending policies, they have addicted every United States government entity of any size that I can think of to these federal dollars. More importantly, they have convinced many of the citizens of the United States that these federal dollars, as they are referred to in nearly any budget discussion, are the only thing that stands between taxpayers and extremely high local taxes. If a small municipal-sized entity were to try to turn down a federal project and the funding that went with it, the local citizens would probably be very unhappy. Since local government officials are accessible to the voters that elected them, the voters could, and probably would, make life very difficult for anyone at the local level that dared not take federal dollars.

The liberals have used our own money against us so effectively, and for so long that we have reached a point now where just the threat of withholding this money will make nearly any local government jump through each and every hoop that the federal government demands. Not only that, but state governments would think long and hard before they behaved any differently.

So ultimately, the leftists in the federal government are using our own money, which they have confiscated from us, to control us. Don't you think now would be a good time to put an end to this immoral practice?

Personal Responsibility

One of the larger components of the left's attack on our society is the steady attempt to erase personal responsibility. To be able to segment our culture, and turn us against each other, they must make sure that the majority of people do not accept blame for the positions they find themselves in or the actions that landed them in difficulties and keep them there. The more people that the liberals have that are dependent on the federal government in some way, the easier it will be for them to maintain and increase the bureaucracies that are supposed to help these "downtrodden", or "victims" as they are often referred to.

Our capitalist society is based on hard work, ingenuity, and perseverance. If you are willing to work hard, use your head, and stick with something, more than likely, success is going to be the result. This goes for nearly any kind of occupation that you can think of.

As our social order used to operate, while an individual might have awakened in the morning, decided life was bad and somebody else was to blame, they would have had a lot of trouble convincing friends and neighbors that they had arrived at a low station in life through no fault of their own. After a lot of complaining, they would have either figured out that maybe they did have some influence over their own destiny, or alternately, that nobody wanted to hear about their troubles and fairly or unfairly (in their own minds) they were going to have to handle life's problems.

As I said, that's how our society used to operate. Now, thanks to a lot of liberal hand holding and coddling, a large part of our society has come to believe that not only are their problems not of their own making, but troubles are actually forced on them by other people. And by golly, these other people owe them something for all of these problems. This doesn't start with adults either, the leftists are smart, and they know that to truly turn people against themselves and get them to live lives that will ultimately be self-destructive, they need to start with them as young as possible.

The federal government has pushed its way into the school systems very aggressively. State governments and local school boards used to struggle with educating their students as well as they could. Now, instead, they struggle to comply with a lot of feel good federal regulations forced on them, and at the same time attempt to educate students. The actual learning part of school is falling further and further behind. Now educators aren't really allowed to interact with pupils, it's more that all of the contact between educators and students is legislated from the federal government, or to help confuse the issue, actually enacted by the state governments, but done so as to be in compliance with federal regulations.

Since all these unwanted and unnecessary regulations result in an unwieldy and inefficient bureaucracy, education costs have skyrocketed. Keeping in compliance with all the top down regulations has driven the cost of public schools through the roof. We spend a shameful amount of money on children in public schools for the declining amount of actual educating that is being done. Unfortunately, between government over regulation and liberal educators unions, the bureaucracy just becomes more and more bloated.

This is just another example of the left killing more than one bird with a single stone. They have turned our educational system into another huge bureaucratic jobs program, and at the same time co-opted that same educational system to their own ends.

Since costs per student are so high, cash strapped communities that are finding this expense more and more burdensome are really taking note of the employee to student ratio. Naturally, this ratio is very poor and at this point in time, school districts seem to have more employees to students, with less of them being teachers than ever before. Local citizens fix on issues like this ratio, along with the high costs of maintenance and construction (that has to be done as mandated by federal standards) and focus the blame on the nearest group that they can find, which is usually the local school board. Local school boards probably get the most blame for school problems and yet have the least regulatory control. This is exactly how the federal government wants it. Infighting and confusion at the local level just gives the left-ists more opportunity to assert control on what is supposed to be a local issue.

The worst part of this frustration with the local school boards is that the group that is bearing the brunt of the blame for declining education, is the one entity that could turn this trend around if they were left to their own devices. There are a few school districts that still have very low dropout rates and turn out well educated students, but they are definitely in the minority, and they are imparting this good education, in spite of the federal government, not with the help of it.

As far as education goes, I can't imagine that a majority of citizens would be, or are happy with a school system that gives their children a mediocre education at best. I think that if the schools were actually under real local control, versus actual federal rule, we would see a vast improvement in the quality of education. Additionally, I think the cost per student would probably decline. Liberals claim to want equal education for every child, but what they are really doing is controlling another segment of our lives and instead of emulating the schools that are doing the best job, they are regulating them and everybody else at the same time to create an average one-size-fits all that greatly limits and frustrates achievers.

It's no secret that charter and private schools can give students a much better education for a lot less money. The reason that they can do this is they actually have influence over the curriculum they are teaching and additionally, latitude on how they go about presenting that material to the students. They also have the option of having troublesome students removed from the school. It's amazing how the possibility of some kind of real discipline straightens up the average student. Order is something that is seriously lacking in the public schools since according to liberals a little discipline might damage some poor child's self esteem.

All the tentacles that the feds have extended into the American public school system have done nothing but dumb down the average education, remove the ability of the teachers and administrators to discipline unruly pupils, and take real control of local schools from the communities that actually have to pay for them. Additionally, and this is probably the most harmful part, they have convinced many or most of the underperforming students, that bad grades are not their fault.

The students take this attitude of "it's not my fault" with them after they leave school. I have met many people in my life who just couldn't seem to get on track and support themselves, and the one quality that they all seem to share is that whatever their problem appears to be, they will all tell you that "it's not really my fault." I don't know if those people picked up that attitude in school or maybe because of some indulgent parent, but either way, whoever taught them that their own problems are not due to their own actions didn't do them any favors.

School is only the beginning of the liberal war on personal responsibility. For the people who didn't manage to get through our school system with enough of a work ethic and determination left to support themselves, well, we have all kinds of public assistance housing and programs to "help them out". Taxpayer financed by the way.

Liberals have managed over the years to use the very real compassion of conservatives to push through all kinds of feel good legislation and programs. Liberals will put through programs that are supposed to help people, but oddly enough, these programs come with large bureaucracies and lots of spending that has to be controlled by the, wait for it, federal government. The arguments that they use to get these things passed are usually along the lines of "it will help a lot of the down trodden" and "only a nazi named Hitler" would vote against it. You would think that after a while, people would get wise to this, but by the time the media gets through spinning it, the liberals will seem like wise elder statesmen and the conservatives will be cast as backward, ungrateful, sniveling, (probably racist) misers.

Think I'm incorrect about the media? At the time of this writing, Congress and Obama are fighting over extending, or not extending the Bush era tax rates. The preceding two sentences are exactly what they are arguing about. If the present tax rates are extended, all that will happen is there will be no income tax rate increase. If they are not extended, there will be an income tax rate increase. However; the media is reporting that Obama is going to give us a tax cut. In fairness, not all of the main stream media is reporting it as an Obama tax cut. Some of them are calling it a plain tax cut, or tax cut extension. None of them are reporting that if it passes, nothing changes. Talk about having the press in your pocket.

The government war on self reliance and responsibility starts as early as possible, but on the other end, for the people that don't manage to gather some true sense of self worth and escape "the system," it can last until the grave.

You would think that once children graduated from high school and got out into what we refer to as the "real world" that they would then figure out that school wasn't so bad, and if you don't start taking care of yourself, it can be a cold, cruel world. That is more or less how it worked for me and my generation. Some of us made the transition to the working world better than others, but for good or bad, we all found out that when you work for people, they expect you to show up on time, pay attention, and get your work done. We also found out during the Carter years that just being willing and able to work didn't necessarily mean that there was going to be a job available. That was a harsh lesson to learn that I and a lot of other people like me survived without government assistance.

Now we are going through hard times and instead of encouraging people to learn how to control their own destiny, we are extending unemployment benefits to ninety nine weeks and more. This is a feel good solution that will give real help to very few people while causing an extensive amount of long term harm.

Extending the unemployment program to cover years instead of a few weeks is just a way of creating another welfare class. This is a real plum for liberals because doing it this way makes dependants out of people who at least once, held an actual paying job. A working class citizen is just the type of person that is liable to not care for liberal agendas. After all, these people used to get paychecks from employers and would have had taxes deducted from those checks.

Looking at the amount that government deducts from your pay tends to make you curious about where that money is going, and when a government funded art program produces something like a crucifix in a bottle of urine, well, somebody (a taxpayer) who is being forced to finance that urine soaked crucifix may make things a little hot for the people giving out the largesse that allowed it.

On the other hand, if the government has convinced this same former tax payer that without the easy and convenient unemployment benefits, they would starve, then there is one more government dependant that won't oppose the leftists. In fairness, I bet that a lot of the people on extended unemployment are there because of the fear of striking out on their own with no safety net. I've been jobless before, and it is indeed a scary place, but as long as the easy solution of perpetual unemployment exists, these people will live in daily fear of losing everything without realizing that they hold the keys to their own independence. This is just the frame of mind that is going to prevent any resistance to the liberal agenda.

Besides the moral decay that overextended unemployment is going to inflict on people that used to be productive taxpayers, doling out these benefits is also going to increase the national debt. I know that conservatives want to use unspent "stimulus funds" to "pay for it", but the fact is, those stimulus funds are also debt, so the argument isn't whether or not this new welfare program is going to increase the debt. The fact of the matter is they are only fighting over how much it is going to increase the debt. This debt increase doesn't matter to the liberals; it just lets them keep on with their programs the same as they have been doing for years and years.

There's no way that liberals don't know how harmful this unemployment extension is going to be in the long term. They are doing this because it gives them more people on the *dole,* and fewer actual taxpayers to fuss about the way our country is being driven into the ground. True conservatives just can't grasp the concept of not being worried about the national debt, so liberals talk about the debt and debt reduction as a smoke screen for their true agenda.

That not very hidden agenda is to remove as much of the sense of personal responsibility from our society as possible. The more people who are willing to deny that they control their own destiny, the more people who aren't going to make a fuss when the federal government steps in to control some facet of their life.

A work ethic and personal responsibility are part of our democratic, capitalist society. Even children of irresponsible parents are going to be exposed to these character traits. Leftists know this, that is why they have extended so much control into the educational system, and more importantly, as they extend their control, they reduce the input of the parents.

A well educated population with a sense of personal responsibility would soon rid itself of a lot of the liberal programs, get spending under control, and generally decrease the power of the federal government. As all of this is the antithesis of what the left stands for, they do everything that they can to prevent it.

Spending Problem

One of the biggest issues, realistically, probably the biggest one, that face us is getting our budget deficit under control, and the national debt paid off. If we can accomplish that, we will improve everything about the United States. Right now, we are engaged in a fierce battle between liberals and conservatives about this very thing, but I'm not sure the conservative side is fully aware of exactly who the enemy is. We still have so called conservative politicians that, even at this late date, want to continue trying to "reach across the aisle" and be bipartisan. The bloated budget of the federal government and getting or not getting it under control is a make or break problem for us. Obama knows this and that is why he is heaping more debt and entitlement spending on us as fast as possible.

I consider it to be mind boggling that at this point in time there are still people in our federal government who appear not to realize that we are in a struggle between two diametrically opposed philosophies that can no longer exist together. Right now it is conservatives versus the liberals and Obama, and the only real choice is which side you are on. Conservatives must pull together and stop the liberal policies that are ruining us, and being "bipartisan" is not going to get that done. Unless the liberals would like to be bipartisan and accommodate the conservatives, you know, kind of like they did for the last two years when the liberal agenda put huge spending bills through against the will of the majority of taxpayers.

The 2010 midterm elections were a very clear indication of what the citizens of the United States want, and how they feel about the last two years. It doesn't take an expert politician to see that the Republicans didn't get elected, instead the democrats were de-elected. Additionally, the Republicans and conservatives that were sent to Washington aren't supposed to be the *party of no*; they are supposed to be the party of ABSOLUTELY NOT. I think that's why so many tea party candidates were elected.

For those of you that think that electing inexperienced tea party candidates is or was a bad thing, let me offer this thought. We have for the most part elected experienced party politicians for years and years, and that is how we got here. I think since we have pretty much proved that the way we have been doing things for the last fifty or sixty years hasn't worked out so well, that maybe it's time to get back to the inexperienced but truly well intentioned citizen legislators that have been successful in their nongovernment job life. Let's get a different kind of person into these offices and turn them into our experienced politicians. Think how much better off we would be if we had a congress filled with hundreds of people that knew how things really work, were aware of how important a budget is, and were competent in their fields before they ever ran for office. I know I would feel a lot better about our government if that were the case.

The liberals are on the side of more spending and more debt. The more money and bureaucracy that they can control, the better they like it. Leftists have no concern with what they are spending or what the ultimate cost of that spending and borrowing will be. As long as they are in control, the printing presses at the mint will run nonstop if that's what it takes to keep them in power.

I know that I go on and on about this, but the fact of the matter is the leftists simply want power, money, and control of the money. They don't care about individual U.S. citizens, the environment, the economy, or any other thing that they say they are compassionate about. Obama completely understands their greed and cupidity, and that is why he has been so successful in harnessing them to his program.

Take a look at Al Gore; he is supposed to be their champion of global warming, in fact he just about invented the issue (but he didn't invent the Internet). If he really cared about global warming, he wouldn't fly everywhere in private jets, have a fleet of SUVs, and live in a house that should properly be labeled a compound (I wonder how many of those carbon capturing trees had to be killed to build his house). Al Gore is little different from all the other leftists that claim support for some issue, as long as they get to dictate and control the cure for that issue. Mr. Gore is just a little more obvious about his private disdain for what he publicly supports.

These issues and any other that they may claim to be concerned about are simply a means to an end. If they really cared about things and wanted to actually identify problems, solve them, and move on to the next one, while at the same time trying to be practical, humane, and realistic, well, then they would be conservatives, wouldn't they?

Recently the 2010 lame duck Congress passed the extension of the existing tax rates. What this means is that the tax rate will remain the same, nothing has increased, and nothing has decreased; there simply is no change. According to the liberals, this is one of the worst things that could possibly have happened. Liberal columnists, commentators, and pundits are railing on and on about what these tax cuts have done, and will do to us.

I even read one columnist that claimed (the Bush tax cuts is how he labeled it) that not only is this extension of the present tax rates going to cost us a lot of money, but these same tax rates have already cost the U.S. Treasury over four trillion dollars since they were first enacted. I won't give what he said there the dignity of calling it a "train of thought", but if you follow the reasoning that he was attempting to grasp, then all we would have to do to solve our present debt problems would be to hold spending at present levels, increase the tax levels to where they were when Clinton left office, and hold that course for about twenty four years. Whew, talk about a good day's work, we just solved one of the worst problems that we have ever faced, and we still have time to move on to some other project. Man, that guy is a deep thinker. The columnist that I mentioned above is just a symptom of the larger problem. The liberals are going to attack anything about the federal budget as a revenue problem. That is how they always frame their arguments and they are very vocal and visible while doing it.

The left is always vociferous about anything to do with taxation. I think that the reason they are so pro-tax is not because of the revenue it might bring in, but about the control that levying taxes gives. If you can tax something, you have power over it. The left is about power much more than they are about revenue.

Start talking about changing tax rates, and you will hear all kinds of things such as increased revenues will mean more money to pay down the debt (Fourteen trillion dollars later, I think we can go ahead and say that doesn't work). Decreases in the tax rate will automatically decrease revenues. Increases in tax rates won't hurt the economy. Decreases in tax rates will decrease revenue and not help the economy. Decreases in tax rates will mean less revenue, we will have to lay off school teachers and close the Washington Monument. I could list a lot of other ways that leftists defend or debate taxes (confiscation of your money), but the fact is they are all arguments that are meant to keep the whole nation looking at and talking about revenue, and specifically not mentioning spending.

The reason they do this is to focus attention away from the real issue. As I have said and will continue to say, the liberals are master manipulators. As long as they shape the argument away from the true issues they will always have an advantage in forwarding their policies.

If the liberals actually cared about revenue, then the amount of revenue taken in would affect spending. If there really was any kind of relationship between actual revenue and what the federal government spends, then we wouldn't be borrowing trillions of dollars at a time.

The true problem that we need to deal with is not revenue. Revenue is certainly an important issue, but the actual problem we have is not one of government income. Our federal government takes in astronomical amounts of money. The money exists to do what the federal government is supposed to be doing, and additionally support a lot of things that we would, as a people, like to do.

What we have is a spending problem. This is where the liberals do not want any attention focused. If you want to hear a really loud outcry, and additionally be called a nazi, start talking about spending cuts. Or even better, propose eliminating some existing programs and/or bureaucratic positions. Any mention at all of anything that is some kind of decrease in spending will draw the full ire of the liberals and their mainstream media lapdogs.

Just to back that up, after the 1994 midterm elections when the Republicans swept into power in the house on the platform of the contract with America, one of the issues that they focused on was the cost of the school lunch program. What the Republicans proposed was an actual increase in the funding for school lunches, but less of an increase than the liberals wanted and not administrated like the left wanted. The press and leftists screamed long and loud about the "cuts" that were going to be imposed on the school lunch program by those mean, nasty Republicans. The actual issue of how much of an increase in funding there would be got very little discussion.

Spending is just one issue among many where the leftists and bureaucrats focus attention on feel good sound bite issues. A lot of smoke and mirrors about conservatives trying to take the food out of the mouths of poor disadvantaged starving children is exactly how the liberals focused notice away from the real issue of trying to curb runaway spending and bureaucracy. In fact, it worked so well that the government is now so deeply involved in feeding school children that nobody would ever give a thought to how much spending it involves or how many government minions are looking after it. Why, Michelle Obama herself has made what our children are eating at school, and pretty much everywhere else, her signature issue.

As a side note on the school lunch issue, when all of this was going on, I had children in elementary school; my wife and I were very active in the PTA, and I knew all the workers at our neighborhood school at least well enough to say hello. With all the hype that was going on in the press about school lunches, I became curious about the actual results in the cafeteria, so I found the lady that was in charge of it and asked her what the end results would be. She told me that some of the children who attended our school were not taken care of at home, and she felt that some of these kids only got two decent meals per day (They served breakfast to students who came in early). She told me in no uncertain terms that no matter what the federal funding level was, in her cafeteria, those children were going to eat. That, my friends, is somebody at the local level who sees a problem and solves it. She identified that there were hungry children, realized that the best solution she could come up with was to feed them so they could study and learn what they need to advance themselves, and made sure it happened. She didn't try to get the parents food stamps, aid to dependent families, or any kind of financial help. She fed, the, children, problem identified, and problem solved, without additional federal intervention or control.

As I keep repeating, the liberals are the best marketers the world has ever seen. Since they are not constrained by any wish to stick to actual facts, and additionally, they usually have a need to guide your attention away from what is really happening, these people have developed methods of seeming to focus on one thing while doing something entirely different that would put Machiavelli to shame.

Where conservatives spend most or a great deal of their time dealing with single issues, trying to get the best possible solution to a problem, or at the very least try to ensure that policies and laws do as little damage as possible, liberals are more of a big picture group. That big picture is more federal control of any and all aspects of our economy and daily life so they can increase their control and power. Defeat a liberal on one issue here, and they will pop up with something else over there. As our federal government is set up now, an occasional loss on spending is only temporary, but any program gains are permanent.

If you still feel that I'm a little overboard in what I say about the left constantly wanting more spending just for the sake of spending, let's take a look at, say, the Department of Education. According to pretty much any liberal that talks about it at all, we are not spending enough money on education. The constant drumbeat from the left and the media is that we aren't spending enough money on our children and as a consequence, they aren't getting the education that they deserve. Often, they come right out and blame this on conservatives, but if they don't, the implication is usually that it's the right's fault. The question is usually something along the lines of, how can these nasty conservatives do this kind of thing, depriving our children of the education they deserve? For shame.

However, as far as I can determine spending on children has steadily increased through the years while at the same time our children's test scores have been declining. So instead of a bunch of cruel conservatives holding our children back, what we actually have is the Department of Education presiding over declining schools while spending more money per capita on students to achieve this decline.

Since even just a halt of the slide in education would be better than the steady decline we have now, how about we give someone else a crack at this?

I'm sure that if you were to publicly float the idea of just doing away with the Department of Education and turning control of schools back to the states and the local school boards (by the way, remember these are the people that are actually having to foot the bill for this declining education, you know, taxpayers) we would immediately be told that the quality of education would decline. To be fair, we should give advice about declining test scores from the Department of Education some thought because over the years they have proven that if there is one thing they know something about, it *is* declining test scores.

The Department of Education is just like any other of a number of federal agencies; their primary product is bureaucrats and government jobs, not properly educated children. Not only does their abysmal record prove that education is not their first concern, but this particular cabinet level agency provides a perfect picture of the non-relationship between revenue, spending, and results at the federal level.

Racism

I think that we can all agree that racism is a bad thing. In fact, our society understands that fact so well, that even the few people that truly are racist go to great lengths to hide that fact from everybody else, or at least everybody that they don't know to be like minded. And by the way, while I'm a WASP, I have spent time in some places where my kind is not wanted, just tolerated. It doesn't matter who you are, there are places in the world where your presence isn't appreciated. Sad, but true.

In fact, many people would say that racism and discrimination are the very worst problems any society, not just ours, can have. As a whole we are so concerned about this issue that we spend untold amounts of money and time trying to eliminate bigotry, or even the possibility of bigotry.

We go about this attempted eradication of discrimination in all kinds of ways. We have done things like forced busing of students from one school to another to attempt to reach some kind of approved ratio of certain races to others which is supposed to bring about equality. You could almost call this reverse racism, except in the busing case, it's still racism, just state sponsored and enforced.

We have had racial quotas for years under the equal opportunity system. The ironic thing about the equal opportunity program is that while it is slowly dying out, where it is still used, it is about everything but equal opportunity. This was and is nothing but a quota system that either heavily encouraged or in some instances forced, acceptance of applications based on little more than a percentage according to the race, gender, or economic class of the applicants.

Think we don't discriminate by economic class? Think that no government agency would separate you out by how much money you make? I will deal with this point further in the next chapter, but for now, if you don't believe the government would hold a grudge against you because of how much money you make, try to put your small children in the Head Start program. You will find out very quickly that if you make any kind of living at all, they will not accept your kids. I'm not talking about wealth either. If you are able to provide basic necessities, the Head Start program will not teach your children. In fact, I checked and in my state, a family of four that makes twenty three thousand dollars a year would be over the income limit for the Head Start program.

Do you realize that with income limits like that, the children that get into Head Start, which is an early learning program, are only going to be the kids of the lowest possible earners, or the children of families on public assistance? Why would anybody want to create a group of only these children and no others? Talk about discrimination and isolated groups. Is it the idea of Head Start to insulate these children from other influences and reinforce public dependency? Even if that isn't the goal, I bet that's what the results are. Oops, sorry, I got sidetracked, back to more about how bad discrimination is.

So let's see, if I remember, it is unethical, illegal, wicked, morally wrong, and depraved to discriminate against anybody because of race, color, creed, ethnicity, social standing, sex, sexual preference, height, weight, age, country of origin, handicap, or any other of a lot of reasons that I've missed here.

Additionally, if I remember all of this correctly, the final arbitrator of who is or isn't practicing discrimination, or who is or isn't being discriminated against is, oh, I know this one, the federal government. The federal government has set itself up as the institution of last resort when it comes to defining or identifying discrimination.

If you are accused of discrimination, either fairly or unfairly, you more than likely are going to be judged according to standards set by the federal government. One of the things that I find very wrong about this is that the only people I see still labeling citizens by race are government entities. Sadly, this also includes my state government, which should have better sense. I can only hope that this compulsory sorting by race is being forced on the state by the federal government.

Every federal form that I have filled out for a long time has very specifically asked my race. If the federal government is so concerned about equal treatment, why does it even want that information? Why would it even occur to someone to ask about race on an application? Who cares what the race is? If discrimination against a person occurs, what race or sex, or age, or etc. they are doesn't make the discrimination better or worse. Additionally, I'm not talking about complaints that are being filed that deal with racism, I'm talking about things like tax returns, and jury cards.

One of the biggest reasons that the feds are so invested in race is that there are huge government bureaucracies that do nothing but deal with race. I bet there are hundreds of thousands or possibly millions of federal bureaucrats that make their living supposedly trying to eliminate racism and establish equality. The only problem is, if equality were ever to be established and bigots became a thing of the past, then they would be out of work. So guess what these bureaucrats find wherever they look hard enough? If you guessed equality and fairness, try again.

I personally believe that we have made huge progress in the struggle against racism. I think that race relations have been improving for years because right minded thinking citizens of all races realize that racism is inherently ignorant, and up to recently, I had expected that trend to continue. Now, since we have been making steady progress, the people that depend on conflict between races have started fomenting the very trouble that they are supposed to be solving.

Government agencies are finding totally new types of discrimination, people like Jessie Jackson (when he can spare the time from philandering) and Al Sharpton not only see bigotry in every situation, if you or anybody else will hold up a microphone (one of the most dangerous places in the world is the spot between Jessie Jackson and a camera) they will be sure and enlighten you on how racism caused whatever event is under discussion. And not just any plain old discrimination either, but the kind that needs submission to the demands of Jessie and Al. I don't actually blame these two or the other people like them on liberals; after all, percentage wise, we are going to be saddled with a few kooks. What I blame on the left is the fact that the political climate is such that people like this get the attention they do without being laughed at.

Obama and the left make frequent use of the race issue. Now that we have a black president, any dissent from the right will quickly be labeled as racist. Liberals have long claimed that the high ground in anything that involves race belongs to them. They do this with the willing cooperation and outright aid of the media. An excellent example of how backward this presentation of leftists as great champions of racial equality is, was the late senator Robert Byrd. As noted earlier, Senator Byrd was a kleagle (recruiter) for the Ku Klux Klan for Pete's sake. He also publicly and repeatedly used the word ^#$^^&, (sorry, I still refuse to print that one), just a few short years before his death. I don't know what exactly it would take to prove that you are a real racist, but I bet that membership in the KKK and that type of language would be accepted as proof in most places. I know I'm convinced.

Personally, I think the leftists admired Robert Byrd as one their best people. The pork barrel projects that he was able to push through are legendary in both size and number. Couple that with the obvious racist history that didn't seem to stick to him, and you have someone that the liberals often held up as a champion of the left.

And before anybody can say, "The conservatives would have done the same thing," let's talk about David Duke. Duke was a member of the KKK who claimed to be a Republican. The Republican Party was embarrassed by him and disowned him as quickly as they could. They certainly didn't forgive his racist ties and help him get elected to national government. In fact, they dropped him so hard and fast, I haven't even heard of him in years.

A really prime example of Obama playing the race card to increase dissent and distract people from his true agenda is the so called "beer summit." The actual reason for the beer summit was supposedly to smooth over the problem created when Obama interjected himself in a dispute between a black college professor and a white policeman. As the story was shaped, Obama had spoken hastily and wrongly blamed the whole problem on the white policeman before he had all the facts and to save face, he had the beer summit and everybody "kissed and made up." The problem with this story as it was told to the public is that you have to assume that the president of the United States is not only less informed about day to day happenings than somebody who watches the evening news, but that additionally all of his advisers are equally ill informed. Seriously, if there is any one person in the world who can say, "I need to get the details on that," and have them almost instantly, it is the president of the United States.

The actual result of the beer summit (intentionally) was to start stirring up racial tension and use it as a tool to keep the electorate divided and on edge. The plan has worked well too. Now, the left is not limited to *nazi* or *Hitler* for pejorative slurs to toss at the right, or really just anybody that disagrees with them. Now they can go to sleep at night with a smile and mumbling the word *racist*.

As I have already said, racism is alive and well in the federal government because the liberals have made sure that it is built into the fabric of the government, and thus many federal workers depend on racism for a living. Again, a very large number of federal employees depend on the war on racism for a source of revenue, and if that "war" is ever won, then they wouldn't be needed and hence, no more job. If there is anybody reading this book who thinks a bureaucracy would finish its work and voluntarily dissolve, might I suggest that you put this book down and look for something in the Marvel line of literature.

The group that is quick to say that any dissent with Obama is racist are the same people that couldn't stand Condoleezza Rice. Condoleezza Rice is generally liked by the conservatives, and usually absolutely loathed by liberals. She is a smart, well spoken, classy, black woman that George W. Bush appointed as his secretary of state. The left pretty much threw a hissy fit every time she spoke, appeared somewhere, or just generally did something. There was absolutely no praise from the left, the supposed champions of equality, for the historic appointment of a black female to the top cabinet post. Instead they spent their time and energy attacking her at every opportunity.

The same liberals that are trying to get any kind of immigration amnesty bill through that they can, while at the same time saying that conservative opposition is racist, are the same group that blocked the appointment of Miguel Estrada to the D.C. Circuit Court of Appeals. Without going into a lot of detail about that shameful episode, Miguel

Estrada was very qualified for the appointment, but the left was concerned that he might be a conservative, so they used political process to block his nomination. For a group that claims to be all about equal opportunity, they are demonstrably not about racial equality. They are about maintaining the power and status that they covet, and that retention of power at any cost is what they do, and they do it with the collaboration of the media. Without a cooperative liberal press, these actions would not withstand the disinfectant properties of the light of day.

So if liberals are really trying to stomp out racism, prejudice, and discrimination, and we have spent all of this time and money on it, why are the people on the left still accusing everybody of being racists? According to them, they've been in charge of the battle, so if we haven't made any headway, can't they at least be a little embarrassed at their lack of progress? Would it be too much to ask for some kind of cost accounting per racist that they have converted? Or at least some indication of how well they are doing and how much more time and money this is going to take?

Okay, just to put a point on it, the liberals, leftists, and Democrats, however you want identify them, were pro slavery (the Republican Party came about in a large part as an antislavery party), and against the civil rights movement. The Republican Party is the party of Lincoln, who by the way is the author of the Emancipation Proclamation. Despite the fact that Obama arrogantly compares himself to Lincoln, our famous sixteenth president was a Republican. Liberals artfully manage to draw notice away from these inconvenient truths by focusing attention away from them, largely by constantly accusing other people of being racist. Again, they couldn't possibly get away with this without the active consent and help of the national press.

So according to the liberals, the fight against racism is extremely important, must be funded, and they have been fighting the good fight to eliminate racism. I personally think that the liberals are very invested in racism, but according to them, they are against prejudice and I do see that they are accusing a lot of people and institutions of being racist. Anyway, let's assume that this conversion to actually being against bigotry instead of pro-bigotry came about right after

Governor Wallace (a Democrat) gave a rousing speech on the steps of the University of Alabama against the desegregation of schools. Interestingly enough, he based his opposition on the platform of states' rights. While I am generally a proponent of state's rights, I would like to note that the South seceded from the union on a platform of states' rights. Of course in that instance, it was mostly the right to own slaves that was in question. Governor Wallace would have been right at home there.

Wallace gave his speech in June of 1963, so if the liberals saw the light right after that and have been engaged in the struggle against prejudice ever since then, that means they have been on this project for over forty five years. That is a long time. According to the liberals, we are still heavily engaged in this struggle and indeed, they are accusing so many people of being racists now that I have to draw the conclusion that they aren't getting very far. After a group has been involved in a project for nearly half a century, there should be tangible results.

I think that the decided lack of results can be explained by only two conclusions. The first conclusion would be that they are just incapable of getting the job done. Basically, this would assume they are just not smart enough to accomplish any real results. The second is that they have no intention of really doing things that would actually have an effect on racism, and that this lack of measurable results is on purpose. So in the end, it's a choice between the liberals being well intentioned but not very smart or, (and this is my take) intentionally not getting any real results while making full use of the money and power they take from the taxpayers for their "supposed" struggle.

The New Racism

In the last chapter, I spent a lot of ink on racism and the liberal agenda that is wrapped up with and hidden inside the supposed "government war on racism."

What I didn't get into is the "new racism." Do you think we are making progress on prejudice and hatred? I believe that we are starting to go backward and in a hurry. I think that in the United States we have discovered a whole new group that we are being encouraged to hate. This encouragement is coming from the federal government and liberals, and in fact, at the time of this writing, you can't turn on a news show of any kind without something (usually bad) being said about this group.

In fact, if I understand the government rhetoric about these particular people that are being singled out, they hold the key for solving all of our issues. And not only could they solve all our problems, they are the root cause of a lot of what we are dealing with now.

It seems to me, that according to the liberals, this group is so bad and has been such a parasite on the United States that they are not just a bunch of ungrateful, unhelpful, and bad people. They are actually such an intentionally evil group that they not only deserve all of the scorn and spite we can heap on them, but we also need to confiscate their property.

Again, my take on what the liberals and their partners in the press are putting out is that there is a group out there so vile, and behaving in a manner that is so harmful to the rest of us that while we normally are against prejudice, this one group really deserves all the hate, bile, scorn, and discrimination that we can heap on them. These people are acting so badly that the usual rules against prejudice don't apply because in this case they have earned it through their truly evil acts.

Who is this group that is so evil? According to the left, it's those dirty, nasty, despicable rich people. The left hates rich people. In fact, the left hates anybody with money. That's really strange because most of the liberals in Congress are actually what the rest of us would call rich. But it's different with them, they are smarter than us, so their money is actually earned, and they deserve it. Why, isn't Harry Reid one of the richer people in the Senate? That means that he must be really smart, because as far as I know, he made his fortune while working in the Senate, and as money goes, there are definitely better paying jobs out there. He must be one savvy investor. Unless, well, surely there wasn't any dishonesty or backroom deals involved. I mean look at Hillary Clinton and what a cracker jack cattle trader she is. Sorry, I got a little side tracked there.

I know that comparing opponents to Hitler or nazis, is really a leftist debate technique, but in this case the similarities are striking and there for the whole world to see, so I'm going to go ahead and point it out. In nazi Germany, Hitler blamed most of the troubles of Germany on the Jews. He and his henchman told the German population at every turn how evil the Jews were, and if they could just get the Jewish people under control, the horrible things that were being perpetuated by them (Jews) on the Germans could be stopped. We all know where this ended up; but oddly, a lot of it got started with the confiscation of the property of the Jewish citizens. Done by their government I might add. I didn't actually realize how similar the way the nazis started off with the Jews was to what is going on in our country right now against "the rich" until I started writing this book.

Before we discuss rich people or the wealthy any further, we need to talk a little bit about who the left is specifying when they use the term *rich* or *wealthy*. The leftists are real masters of misdirection, and the people they want you to think of when they use these terms or something synonymous is a person along the lines of Bill Gates, or Warren Buffet (by the way, the joke is on Warren Buffet, he was an Obama supporter). Be that as it may, they are right now trying to define wealthy as making over two hundred and fifty thousand dollars a year. So if you make that amount or more, when you hear liberals talking about a tax on the wealthy, well, I have some bad news for you.

Over the background noise of how evil the rich are, liberals try to convince everybody that the rich don't need that much money, aren't job creators, and they (the rich) need to pay their fair share. There is so much wrong with these statements that they need to be dealt with separately.

The argument that the wealthy don't need that much money sounds okay on the face of it, but the fact of the matter is that it is their money. It's not your money, my money, or the government's money. Also, it doesn't matter if they inherited lots of money or earned a pile of it. The facts are that unless they stole it or received it through some criminal enterprise, it's theirs. So if it belongs to the rich, and we vote to take it away, we aren't doing anything but confiscating somebody else's property. Don't misunderstand, as unpleasant of a fact as it may be, there must be some way of collecting revenue for the government, and that means there are going to be taxes. That also means that people with more money are going to pay more taxes. All of that is a fact, but calling it something other than confiscation is incorrect. Additionally, raising taxes on rich people just because they are rich and emotionally it feels good smacks of discrimination. Government encouraged and enforced discrimination at that.

One more point about government enforcement, as much as leftists claim to hate guns (actually, the liberals don't hate guns, they just hate you having guns), when the government takes something from you, if you refuse to the point of physical resistance, you will meet the men with the guns. So when the federal government deprives you or anybody else of property in any form, it is always with the veiled threat of taking it at gunpoint if necessary.

The rich have been so reviled in the United States that any politician that is seen to in any way support even basic rights for the wealthy is smeared loudly and publicly. The few conservative politicians that actually have the guts to stand up for people with money, then have to defend themselves from the perceived guilt of protecting the rich. The wealthy are so despised that just trying to ensure that they get a fair shake (otherwise known as equal representation) is not seen as a good enough reason for a legislator to lower themselves to such a morally low level as to actually be representing the interests of the well to do. The way that most lawmakers present this defense to their inflamed voters is by saying that the wealthy are job creators and we need them. In fact, it is true that people with money create jobs, and if they didn't exist we would have to invent them. It's a shame that our government has turned the wealthy into a class of sub humans that must be hated and any association, or fair dealings with them has to be justified.

In fact, there is no question that the rich create jobs. While the left rails long and loud against this concept, the reality is that most people got wealthy by creating things and hiring other people to help them with that creation and wealth accumulation. If you look into it, a lot of people became wealthy while helping someone else or a group of people get rich. Our capitalist society rewards hard work and good ideas, and the form of that reward is wealth and security. The effects of these good ideas and hard work can be very wide spread.

For an excellent, very well known case in point, let's use Bill Gates and the Microsoft Corporation. Before I go any further, I hope that Mr. Gates is not offended by being pointed out as a shining example of the best that freedom and capitalism can create, but I'm a huge admirer of what he has done and how he lives his life. Most people are familiar with the fact that Bill Gates took an idea, applied hard work and intelligence to it, and built that idea and work ethic into the present day Microsoft Corporation that we are familiar with. He has certainly been financially rewarded for his efforts, but what doesn't get nearly as much attention is how the rest of the nation, and a large chunk of the world, have also benefited from his acumen.

I do most of my paperwork and writing on a computer that runs on the windows platform. I have the use of the best that the Microsoft has to offer. For a few hundred dollars, I can multiply my productivity and save valuable time by using the products that Bill Gates has for sale. My purchase of his software benefits both of us. His company receives the revenue generated by sales to me and people like me, and I can work faster, smoother, and more efficiently. When was the last time you typed a letter on an actual typewriter? Why don't we use typewriters anymore? We don't use typewriters anymore because they are slow, very limited in what they do, difficult to use, and above all, they don't multi-task. Nobody even manufactures typewriters now. If you have one it is an antique, the only question is how old an antique. My computer with windows is capable of so many functions that I don't even have a clue what they all are. If Mr. Gates had not had some incentive to pursue his dreams and ideas, our world would not be nearly as productive as it is now.

Bill Gates and the Microsoft Corporation have helped, and continue to help tens of millions of people to create wealth. I just don't understand how Mr. Gates becoming ultra rich has been anything but beneficial to our country.

While I have singled Bill Gates out as an example of how wealthy people can be, and are beneficial to our economy, there are a lot of other people out there who through their personal journey to financial security have benefited the rest of us. Mr. Gates is probably one of the best known examples, but he is just one among many.

I fail to see how confiscating money from entrepreneurial wealth creators, with proven track records of job creation, and giving it to the federal government is going to benefit the overall economy. Don't forget, the federal government designed the low flush toilet, the curly light bulb, and as I pointed out in the previous chapter, has been failing at the fight against racism for over forty five years. Do you really think the feds are going to use that money better than the people that create wealth for a living?

As far as job creation is concerned, looking at the abysmal record of the federal government concerning creating good nongovernment jobs, I'm going to go ahead and bet on the rich people.

As I mentioned above, one of the points that the left keeps bringing up when discussing the wealthy and why we need to confiscate more money from them is that they "need to pay their fair share." That is a sound bite type of phrase that sounds good in a speech or sixty second spot on the evening news, but doesn't actually stand up to examination. One problem is that whoever is doing the talking also wants to be the one that defines how much is "a fair share." That doesn't seem very "fair" to me.

The only proposals that I have ever heard of where fair, tax, and a defined amount are all involved is in the fair tax proposal that floats around from time to time. Usually these types of proposals just specify a certain percentage of income tax across the board for everybody, or some kind of national sales tax that would move government revenue from the earning side to the consumption side. Liberals are not proponents of either of these two methods of taxation. When you hear a liberal say somebody needs to pay their "fair share," go ahead and substitute the word *more* for fair share, and you will get the gist of it.

The wealthy people that the left wants to take more money from (so the they can have more money to mismanage) are already paying more taxes than the rest of us. A lot more. If a person with a million dollar a year income is paying twenty percent in taxes at the end of the year, that is two hundred thousand dollars. Not only is that a lot more than the rest of us are paying, if that so called millionaire is generating that income by running a business, then all his or her employees are being supported by that business and paying taxes from their wages also. Looks to me like the wealthy people the liberals hate so badly are doing a lot of good things for the United States.

If the liberals had legitimate reason to appeal to the general public for higher taxes, they would be able to present it in a reasoned, calm manner. Since instead they present their proposals for higher taxes in the language of divisiveness and loathing, I think they just show that they have a hidden agenda.

Evil Corporations

Liberals view taxpayers as a group to be ruled, controlled, and robbed. As I have pointed out, a very large part of how they accomplish this goal is by misdirection, no professional magician has anything on a true leftist when it comes to smoke and mirrors. If taxpayers or conservative politicians even sound like they might start talking about wasteful spending, the leftists will be quick to open up some kind of dialogue about revenue.

If shouting about revenue doesn't serve to refocus attention away from spending, then the next talking point will probably be something like the spending in question is going to help poor people. That is, it would if the unfair, hard hearted, nazi-like, racist conservatives would just go away and stop questioning the well meaning bureaucrats who control the entitlement programs.

If even all of that doesn't work, well, there's always time to talk about how those nasty, spiteful, greedy rich people are ruining the United States and costing all the other taxpayers tons of money by refusing to allow all or a very large portion of their built up wealth to be confiscated.

Usually, after all of the above steps have been taken, the political argument has gone so far afield that nothing useful will come of it even if the conservatives are still trying to pursue the truth at this point. As conservative as I am and as much as I like and back the few true conservative lawmakers that we are going to have to depend on to save us, I am frequently frustrated at how often they allow the liberals to frame whatever is under debate however the left would like.

Starting off trying to tame federal spending and ending up debating "tax cuts for the rich" is a win for the left and a loss for the United States. To my way of thinking, starting off trying to cut spending and ending up with a list of entitlement or other useless programs that are going to be cut and/or eliminated (can you say Department of Education?) would be a much better outcome, but somehow, we never seem to get that result.

There is one more fallback position that the left has, and will use if they still need something more to distract the average conservative voter; in fact they like this issue so much that they usually trot it out anytime revenues are under public discussion. The subject I'm talking about is what the average liberal likes to think of as "the evil corporation."

As far as I can tell, the liberals want you to think that the corporations that exist in the United States are big, fat, bloated, money hoarding, tax dodging, society robbing businesses that are not only bad in their own right, but are probably also owned by those nasty rich people. If that isn't what they are pushing, I can't tell it from their rhetoric about taxing these entities, which is usually framed in some version of "If we do this, we won't have to raise taxes on the average taxpayer, but if we don't tax the corporations, a tax increase on individuals is inevitable."

Hey, it just occurred to me, if we can soak these evil corporations for more money, instead of just taxing them to increase revenue, as the left continually suggests, why, we could lower taxes on citizens. The left is always using the threat of a tax increase on citizens if they aren't allowed to tax these evil businesses, so if these corporations are the untapped source of federal revenue that the left seems to be saying they are, why haven't they suggested that we obtain that money and lower the tax burden on people? Maybe it just hasn't occurred to them yet? Actually, I'm a little surprised that they aren't out there proposing this right now while planning to raise corporate taxes on the promise to reduce income taxes, and then just "forget" to lower the income taxes. When the outcry starts over the failure to reduce income tax, then we could go right back to talking about revenue again.

Before you say that last point is just silly, the reason that they aren't out there saying something like that is because it is just ridiculous and even the liberals wouldn't try something that ludicrous. Remember, Nancy Pelosi was in all the national news outlets recently publicly proclaiming that paying people to not work (unemployment insurance extensions) creates jobs. If the left will publicly say that, they will say anything. The only thing that comes to mind that could possibly be more ridiculous than Nancy Pelosi claiming unemployment benefits create jobs would be if Barack Hussein Obama, the father of the largest (unnecessary and harmful) spending bills the world has ever seen, were to start talking about getting the deficit under control. Since he is indeed doing that, and one of the methods that has been put forward (by the left, of course) to tame the deficit is to raise taxes on corporations to increase revenue so we can decrease the deficit. I'm starting to think that I've heard all of this a few times before, and I'm beginning to sense a pattern.

Anyway, if you listen to the liberals, and since they have the press in their pocket it's difficult to avoid hearing them, then it would be hard to think of corporations as anything but soulless commercial entities with hugely overpaid CEOs that would sell their own grandmothers for any kind of advantage. I mean after all, aren't these the huge multinational companies that are moving all their jobs and money overseas?

Some of the leftists politicians in the federal government are very wealthy, and some have partial ownership of corporations, but other than themselves and their own companies or interests, the left likes wealthy people and corporations about the same, which is to say, they intensely dislike both of them (again other than themselves and what they personally own).

Corporations are entities that started off somewhere on a small scale, applied good ideas, and hard work in the proper amounts and turned that into money, or income. Just exactly what the American capitalist society is supposed to foster.

I think that we could all agree that General Electric is a huge multi-national corporation. I bet that it has employees or at least representatives in the majority of the countries of the world. I would also assume that it does a lot of banking that isn't in the United States. Isn't this just the type of business that the left is referring to when they talk about giant corporations? How could a company this large possibly be an example of our democratic, capitalist system? The fact of the matter is that if you go back to the roots of General Electric and try to figure out exactly how it started, it won't take you long to come up with Thomas Edison. Now there was a guy who definitely participated in what capitalism has to offer. Talk about applying hard work and good ideas in large (I almost said *liberal* doses, but I doubt there was much that was liberal about Mr. Edison) amounts. If Thomas Edison isn't the poster boy for the capitalist system, he should be. Say, he also invented the incandescent light bulb, maybe that explains why liberals don't like GE?

At the time of this writing, General Electric has tied itself very closely to the Obama Administration. It is being widely reported in the press that GE paid no income tax this past year and has taken advantage of every political and "loophole" opportunity available to avoid "paying its fair share." At this point in time, GE finds itself in the unusual position of being semi-aligned with the left, reviled more than normal in the press, and gradually losing favor with the general public. This is just another instance of the appearance of a situation being very different from what's really happening. In this case, it looks like a large corporation is making use of existing loopholes to "put one over" on the United States

I think what's actually happening is that we have a political situation that is either allowing a large business to align itself with the people in power, or maybe the people who run GE are afraid of the federal government (looking at GM, Chrysler, and/or large banks, and how the federal government handled them could sure create a lot of unease at GE). It may be that GE has simply made a business decision to try and appease the left and use this method to keep the federal government out of its business.

Whatever the reason for the closeness of GE and the left, there are two things that stand out to me about it. First, in my opinion, Thomas Edison would vehemently disapprove. Secondly, and to me the most disheartening, is that nobody is noting that this voluntary "quasi-melding" of GE and our national government is not how either government or business should be behaving. The fact that the general public is only noting the taxes that GE is or isn't paying instead of the subversion of both business and government is a sad commentary on our political awareness and business acumen (or lack thereof).

Despite all the hyperbole about large multinational corporations that are unethically hiding taxable money from the poor U.S. taxpayer, the actual facts regarding what corporations really are and whether or not they are paying taxes are very different from what the left wants the public to believe.

While the liberals spend a lot of time trying to convince the average American voter that corporations are pretty much the same as those despicable rich people, except on a larger scale, the essentials of what these companies are and how they operate are of course very different from the propaganda the left puts out. In fact, when you listen to a liberal talk about big business, there is almost always one thing that is missing from their speech. They leave this one item out so often that I have come up with a pet name for it. I like to refer to what leftists leave out of their rhetoric on business as a little something which I refer to as *the truth*.

Not that liberals are all that scared of the truth, they will sometimes tell the truth when it suits them. They also occasionally let the reality of what they are up to slip out, but when they do, their coconspirators in the press will give them a pass and not draw undue attention to it.

Corporations are merely legal entities that are set up to do business. The difference between the yard service that mows your yard and a huge multinational corporation is only in complexity and scale, they are both in business, and, this is the most important part, they both have to make a profit.

Liberals in particular, and definitely Obama specifically, have done their level best to try and convince the masses that *profit* is a dirty word. In fact, not that long ago, Hillary Clinton, speaking about a large corporation that had made a five billion dollar profit, said that if she were in power she would take (confiscate) that money. I don't have the exact quote, but the implication was that she would have the federal government take that money away from the entity that earned it, and spend (waste) it on government projects instead. Of course, I could be wrong about what she wanted to do with it; after all, she might have meant that she wanted to invest it in cattle futures.

There are several points that I would like to make about Ms. Clinton speaking publicly about confiscating someone else's money. First this was before Obama came to power and really started personally denigrating companies that make a profit. That just shows you both how far the liberals had already progressed in their attacks on business, and it's a perfect example of how Obama has taken over the leftist program, ramped it up, and turned it to his own uses. Second, the press gave her incredible statement much less attention than it deserved, and when they did, the coverage was mostly complimentary, which really shows the liberal bias of the press. Third, and this is bad, the majority of the general public that did have their attention drawn to it, seemed to either have no real reaction or to actually think it was a good idea.

The left would have you believe that taxing corporations is a painless way of generating revenue for the federal government. They would also like for you to think that the only reason that we aren't getting the tax money from these shady operations that we should is because corporations are owned by rich people with lots of influence and that there are additionally a lot of lobbyists that help keep these organizations from paying the proper amount of taxes.

The truth, that is the part that the left usually leaves out about corporations, is that as I already said, they are just businesses. Corporations are not *evil* and are in business to make money for their owners or shareholders. There is nothing bad about making profits, and in fact, that is the main reason that corporations exist in the first place. If you own any mutual funds or stocks, then you probably are part owner of one or several of these corporations, and I'm sure that you would like to get some return (profit) on your investment. To give you a profit, or dividend, these companies that you own shares in are going to have to bring in more money than they spend.

In America, we call bringing in more money than it costs to operate *profit*. Not only is profit desirable and the reason that businesses exist in the first place, they are an absolute necessity. Being in business and not generating enough revenue to post a profit is called a hobby. At some point, companies that cannot generate net income will cease to exist, period. I just can't stress this enough: companies must make money, and they must return profit or dividends to their owner/share-holders or cease to exist. Of course liberals know this, many of them have and are participating in investment for profit enterprise and made a lot of money doing it. They just "forget" to mention that when they are talking about "profiteering by corporations."

Just like wealthy people, businesses employ people to help them in their attempt to make profits. The company that I referred to earlier that made a five billion dollar profit, not only returned money to their investors, just as it is morally obligated to do, but it probably paid tens of thousands of people (employees and suppliers) to help it do that. Profitable companies have employees that get paid, they buy materials from other companies that also have employees that get paid, and those suppliers also buy from yet other suppliers and contractors that, wait for it, have employees that get paid. These are all non-government, private sector jobs which means that the people that hold them are more than likely taxpayers.

Before we go any further, this is where a leftist will almost always say something like "What about companies like Enron and people such as Bernie Madoff? Weren't they dishonest?" The answer to that is, of course, yes. They were, and are, a bunch of crooks. These were dishonest, corrupt people who ran their companies in an illegal, un-ethical, and immoral manner. Isolated examples like that don't mean that all corporations or investment firms are bad anymore than one corrupt liberal senator means that all liber..., okay, maybe I mean the fact that just because some dogs will bite doesn't mean all dogs are mean or vicious.

So if corporations, whether multinational or not, are huge job generators and employers that return profit on investment for their owner/shareholders, why does the left denigrate them so harshly and try to heavily tax them?

Mostly I think the left is vocal about taxing corporations for two reasons: one, the power to tax is the power to control, and they definitely would like to control as much of our economy as possible, and two, it's just another distraction technique to keep attention away from the real issues. Remember, if there is one thing the left can't afford, it is clear, undistracted attention to what our federal government is up to.

One more very important detail missing from the anti-corporate propaganda is the fact that any taxes that are levied on corporations or other forms of businesses are an expense that has to be figured into the price they charge for their products. This means that all taxes levied on business are passed straight to the consumer (you). I think that most people are aware of this, but to put it into its simplest form, if you decide that the lawn mowing business we referred to earlier should be taxed on its revenue in the amount of ten dollars per yard, the cost its customers will pay just went up. The amount of increase will have to be at least ten dollars plus the overhead costs our intrepid lawnmower incurs keeping up with the reports and forwarding the money to the taxing authority.

So, the next time a professional politician proposes taxing business as a method of "tax relief" for the poor taxpayer, keep in mind that you as a consumer will pay that extra tax only it will be hidden from you in the price of the goods you purchase.

The War on Poverty

One of the biggest weapons that the left is using against our society is the so-called "war on poverty." While the war on poverty has some fairly specific starting programs in the mid sixties, the term has really come to mean anything that is supposed to help the poor become "not poor." I say supposed to help them, because all of the assistance programs and money that has been spent on and in this "war" doesn't seem to have resulted in a victory, or for that matter even anything that resembles a draw. Nevertheless, when leftists talk about socialist programs, you are supposed to think warm thoughts about how we have a lot of government programs in place that are going to help the downtrodden. What you aren't supposed to do is think any further than those warm thoughts and wonder anything like, "what do these programs cost, who's paying for all of this, who's actually in charge", and this is the one you really aren't meant to ask, "how much progress are we making"?

Many of the big entitlement programs are either part of the theoretical war on poverty, or closely associated with it somehow. The reasoning behind these programs was that they were designed to help people who, somehow, through no fault of their own, found themselves in need of a helping hand. These plans also were initially meant to, or were soon expanded to, include people who were needy, but because of some kind of physical (age, infirmity, birth defect, etc.) or mental problem, would not be able to get by without assistance.

From the conservative point of view, there has been no progress in the war on poverty, in fact, it looks to me like whoever the opponent in this particular battle is, they are winning and our side is retreating.

That's my conservative take on the state of the war on poverty between *us* and the other side. From the liberal point of view, the struggle is going great. Leftists have managed to create multi-generational dependants that are almost always going to vote for the person that promises to dole out the most government largesse. They have formed whole new categories of people that look to the federal government to relieve them of all responsibilities and just generally maintain the status quo that they have come to look on as their "right."

The numerous agencies that have been created to handle the money and programs for this "war" have given rise to massive bureaucracies full of liberals. These bureaucratic jobs and what they stand for are going to be much more attractive to liberals than conservatives. Stacking socially progressive bureaucracies with leftists pretty much ensures that these organizations are going to be big spending, self sustaining, and most importantly, ineffective.

I don't have any way of ascertaining this, but I bet that a very large majority of the people that actually staff these organizations that "work with the poor" are liberals. I just don't see a lot of conservatives being interested in this kind of work. I also don't see how a bunch of conservatives could fail at this work as successfully as the liberals that are doing it now. It takes real dedication to not succeed for as long as these programs have been not working. As a conservative, I just don't think that I could work up (or not work up) that kind of determination to fail. Additionally, after I had been failing at something with someone else's money for over forty years, the feelings of guilt would probably overwhelm me.

Not to say that conservatives aren't interested in helping the poor. Conservatives are very interested in helping the poor, but what we aren't invested in is keeping them poor. We try to give actual help that will boost people up, not the perceived help of the liberal that keeps the poor down. I think that if these bloated bureaucracies started hiring conservatives and letting them actually try to help the poor, then we would soon have fewer poor people and more productive taxpayers.

Instead of raising poor families up to the middle class, the war on poverty is not only encouraging poor people to remain poor, it is slowly dragging the middle class down. So instead of the gains that the poor were supposed to make as a result of government "help," assistance that was supposed to turn them into producers and part of the middle class, what is really being accomplished is a watering down of the middle class. Because of this, percentage wise, we have more poor and fewer middle class citizens than we should have.

What's going on may be named "the war on poverty," but instead of the named goal of raising the poor out of poverty, we really have a war on the poor and the American taxpayers at the same time.

Instead of turning poor neighborhoods into areas of hope and improvement, we have turned many inner city areas into crime ridden "hoods" that in some cities even the police are unwilling to enter.

Life in these government provided housing developments and in the federally encouraged ghettos, has become so mind numbing and soul destroying that when an occasional person, be they child or adult, manages to actually leave that background behind and improve their lifestyle, they often refer to it as escaping.

Escape is a term that would be appropriate if you left a prisoner of war camp, or prison. When people use the word *escape* to talk about getting out of a housing project, well, I think that says a lot about housing projects.

Speaking of prison, there is no doubt in my mind that a large part of the prisoners in our jails are there because of how they didn't learn to live law abiding, moral lives while living under the liberal influence of all these "aid" programs. This is where the left gets the conservatives again. Instead of accepting any responsibility for the high crime rate of their socially dependant class, what they do is say that the prisons are so full because of the harsh penalties conservatives insist on imposing. Then, to add insult to injury, they say that the high numbers of minorities, and particularly blacks that are incarcerated are because we are racists.

All the damage that the liberals are doing to the middle class and the poor, which by the way is very harmful to the United States overall, is done in the name of good intentions. The left wants us to believe that they are confiscating money from people that have it, then using it in a manner that provably is harmful to the very people that they claim to have compassion for because, of course, leftist policies are well intentioned.

I fail to see how anyone can do what the liberals have done and truly believe that they are helping people. I'm sorry; I just can't believe a whopper like that. As I have said and continue to say, all of this damage is intentional. It's done in the name of keeping the liberals in power, and that is what they've been doing with the war on poverty since its inception, and if we don't stop this nonsense, we will just get more of the same.

Not only do we owe it to ourselves to get this situation under control, we have a Christian duty and societal obligation to salvage the people who can be helped and save the future generations that will be ruined if these policies are not stopped. The human damage that is being done is wasteful, unnecessary, and cruel. The money that the liberals so crave and are using to destroy people could actually be used to benefit society, if it were to be properly utilized. Since liberals obviously are not going to change all of this, conservatives must.

When the liberals point at the squalor and misery that these permanent government dependants live in, and say it is the conservatives' fault, they are correct, but not for the reasons that the liberals put forth. The liberals say that these conditions exist because we aren't helping these people with enough government assistance or programs, and that if we would just do more, these people would do better. The implication of this being that conservatives are standing in the way of the additional funding that would turn everything into sweetness and light.

The reason conservatives are actually at fault and are indeed partly responsible for the ongoing human misery that these government entitlement programs create is that we have not stepped up to the plate and stopped the liberals from ruining so many people. Our inaction has allowed the left to ruin a lot of lives.

Liberals like to point at the war in Iraq (with mind numbing frequency) and talk about the money and lives that have been spent on it with what they say are no real results. (They mean other than removing a sadistic dictator, freeing millions of people, trying to grow a fledgling democ—. Sorry, sidetracked again). To gain a little perspective on that, at the time of this writing, the liberals have been leading the charge in the fight on poverty and racism for over forty years. This means that if we were to apply the same non winning techniques in Iraq, we would be able to fight there until the year 2043 before we had wasted as much time there as the liberals have in the wars on racism and poverty. I would like a clear victory in Iraq and orderly withdrawal leaving a stable government as much as anybody else, but it seems a bit odd that the leftists are the ones saying that we have had more than enough time to accomplish that. Since I haven't known of any liberal programs that successfully finished and then shut down, I'm not sure what makes them think that they should know how long is *long enough*.

Even though leftists like to talk about the cost of the Iraq war, they are a little less likely to talk about the total cost of the war on poverty. This failed war has cost us so much money and so many wasted lives, that I honestly don't think it can be calculated. We have spent an untold number of dollars that were supposed to turn poor, dependant people into productive, taxpayers, but instead we have taken away any incentive for personal improvement and basically enslaved the poor for political purposes. The damage the liberals have done to poor families in general and the poor blacks in particular is well documented. I think the astronomic rise in single poor mothers can be laid directly at the feet of the liberals. The more dollars and liberal policies that the left applies to this situation, the worse it gets.

Albert Einstein once said, "The definition of insanity is doing the same thing over and over again and expecting different results." So it would seem that since we aren't getting anywhere, throwing more money and bureaucrats at this problem every year would be insane.

As this state of affairs gets worse, instead of the liberals admitting that they have mishandled it, and they need to change how they operate, they demand more money and more people because, after all, can't you see we have a bad problem here and something needs to be done about it? This continual increase of money and people is the actual goal of the war on poverty. Any program that actually decreased the number of people on public assistance and needed less money and bureaucrats every year would be done away with or changed before it could have any real effect.

Any general, secretary of defense, or chairman of the chiefs of staff that handled a war this badly would be publicly fired, and rightly so. Since the left's actual goal is the increasing amount of money that is spent on this failed policy, they continue business (with increases) as usual annually and do not welcome any questions of or investigation into whether or not they are making progress. Any questioning of the expense of these policies is met with immediate attack. As usual the attack will sound something like "Only a nazi or someone named Hitler would even think of cutting this program you racist" (I know, blah, blah, blah, but that is one of ways that the left often responds to anyone that wants to discuss actual facts.)

The leftists' aim is to maintain and increase the spending and number of bureaucrats that are involved in the so called "war on poverty" by appealing to the ingrained (which, by the way is part of our Christian heritage) American kindness and generosity. Any proposed spending cut, or even a proposed increase that is not the amount of increased spending that the left wants, will generate lots of heated talk about the harm to children and the disabled.

The liberal war on poverty is a dismal, visible, humanity wasting, costly, society destroying failure. Isn't it about time we stopped this federal leviathan and instead really helped the poor help themselves out of poverty?

Christianity Under Assault

The Christian religion is under assault in the United States. This assault is both intentional, and of long standing. The progressives use every available weapon to steadily chip away at the Christian foundation that our country is built on.

The further the left can divide people and government from the Christian religion, the more power and control of the populace they will have. The further involved in Christianity and the Bible Americans become, the harder they will resist the liberal progressive control of their lives and wallets.

The leftist attempt to completely remove Christianity from the federal government is actually just a part of the attack on Christianity as a whole. Liberals definitely want to do away with any mention of God, Christ, or anything to do with our Judeo-Christian religions, but the ultimate dream goal for them is to get rid of Christianity entirely. The way of life that the left would like to guide us into, and Christianity, cannot exist side by side. One or the other has to go. (Since I'm a conservative who is also a Christian, guess which one I choose?)

The often touted "separation between Church and State" is not actually written in the Constitution. The first amendment states "Congress shall make no law respecting an establishment of religion, or prohibiting the free exercise thereof." That is a long way from it being unconstitutional to pray publicly, display the Ten Commandments, have Under God in the Pledge of Allegiance, or etc.

As much as liberals try to deny it, the United States of America is a Judeo Christian nation, and that heritage has made us what we are. We would not have been able to reach the heights we have without the Christian foundation on which the country was built, and if the left is able to finally, totally, separate our government from that religious heritage, we will not be able to recover from our present problems.

Obama knows this, so when he says we are no longer a Christian nation, he is voicing one of his fondest wishes.

The flip side of that same coin is that if we will once again acknowledge our true Christian heritage and return to the principles that the left has so successfully guided us away from, we will discover that almost all of our problems are not only of our own making, but also solvable. Facing our societal problems in a moral, responsible manner will be a big step in the direction of resolving them. At present, the left encourages us to leave everything to the federal government. As long as we let the liberals run things as they like, no problems are going to be solved, our present situation is going to worsen, and deep down, we as Christians and/or conservatives know this.

Of course a lot of the road to redemption is going to involve a return to personal responsibility, which certainly means limiting or removing a lot of liberal programs and the entrenched bureaucrats that oversee them. Since the left is all about more control, and more bureaucrats to wield that influence, a little thought will reveal one of the big reasons that they fear Christianity so much.

Do you think that I'm way off base saying that Christianity is under attack? Let's look at some of the ways that assault is carried out; first, there is no such thing as a "Religious Right." This label is meant to imply a group of right wing religious zealots that would like to see the United States turned into a Christian theocracy by any means possible. This term is often used when describing *militias*, which if we are to believe the press, are just popping up everywhere. They like to blend the "religious right" and "militias" together as much as possible because that way they are attacking "God and guns" at the same time, two things that the left truly hates. Despite what the press and liberals would like us to think religious right means, when they use this term, they are really talking about all Christians, and additionally, they are trying to cast Christians as a group of lunatics that nobody should ever listen to, or be a part of. In fact, the continual reference to the religious right is designed to embarrass Christians and help silence them. After all, if there really was a group that truly could be labeled the Religious Right, then that would mean there must be a "Religious Left", and even a group of "Religious Moderates". I'm not aware of any substantive talk about the existence of either the religious left or moderates. What little mention of groups like this that does exist is almost always made by individuals (usually liberal politicians or someone in the media) who are speaking as people who have put themselves apart from Christianity.

Liberals in general and Obama in particular fear Christianity, and Christians. The liberal agenda cannot stand up to Christian principles and as I already said, Obama's sympathies either lie with the Muslim world or at the very least, are not with Christians. The liberal agenda is the antithesis of Christianity and the Christian Bible. While leftists claim to be helping the downtrodden, what they actually are doing is enslaving them. The Bible is very clear that helping others is a duty to God. That same Bible is also clear that aid to others is to be in a form that actually helps them to prosper and become better people. The Bible teaches a duty to help people so that they may improve their lives and thus be able to help others. It is also the obligation of Christians to lead (not force) people to God by example and faith.

The way our government "helps" our citizens not only does not urge people to better themselves, it actively and intentionally discourages personal improvement. A moral, principled, self supporting electorate is not going to be in favor of liberal policies that encourage multi-generational welfare, repeat criminal offenders, confiscatory taxes, and the squandering of money on people who could help themselves, but won't.

As in most things, this attack on the important Christian bedrock of the United States is carried out with the cooperation and complicity of the main stream media. As a case in point of this very obvious collaboration, let's take a look at the Westboro Baptist Church.

The Westboro Baptist Church is a shameless organization of loony wing nuts that gather together to protest at the funerals of service personnel who have been killed in Afghanistan and Iraq. I can't say enough bad things about this group of idiots. Nothing I'm going to be able to come up with here will even come close to describing how despicable and inhuman their behavior is. While I think that most people, and especially most true Christians would agree with my opinion, the media uses the antics of this misguided group to further denigrate

B Kreitler

Christians. They give this group a lot more press than they deserve, and will generally note their inappropriate behavior while emphasizing that they are a Christian (Baptist) group. I have even seen them referred to in print as a "conservative religious group."

Liberals, and their coconspirators in the media, don't spend so much time and effort attacking the Jewish and Christian religions just because they don't like them. While they may find our Judeo Christian heritage to be an irritating fact that, no matter how they try they can't quite separate us from. The fact of the matter is, for them to succeed in their agenda, they must defeat our Christian principles.

Remember, the liberals are a group that is behind government funded abortions, yet despises the death penalty. They don't just believe in killing unborn children, they encourage it. Yet at the same time they claim the lives of our most heinous criminals are sacrosanct. This is also the group that tries to extend all the protections of our Constitution and the Geneva Convention to terrorists, while prosecuting some of our own soldiers for shooting these same terrorists on the battlefield. Not to belabor the point, but the left is the group that is very strenuously trying to bring us death panels. Think about it, under unrestricted liberalism, the son of Sam killer would be safe, but Grandma better watch out.

The examples that I have pointed out above, should make it perfectly clear that liberals don't actually have principles. What they call principles are merely the issues that they use to get the one thing that they care so deeply about. As I have said over and over and over again, that one thing is power. A return to Christianity and Christian principles would remove or severely limit that power. The fact that with a return to Christian principles a lot of societal ills would be reduced is not important to the left. What is important to them is that a return to personal responsibility and Christian principles would put the liberals out of power. Staying in, and increasing their control of power is all they care about. If supporting government funded deaths of unborn children and prosecution of innocent American military personnel will help them keep their authority, they will do it and not lose a minute of sleep over it.

One common and heavily used method of attack is to constantly tell the American citizens that our Founding Fathers were not actually Christians, and since they weren't Christians, then they couldn't possibly have meant for the country they built to be a Christian nation. Therefore, any references to Christianity, God, and Christian principles that did get into our founding documents (according to the liberals) are not really meant to indicate that we are a Christian nation. That is, of course, a lot of bunk, the Founders were Christians, and the references to God and Christianity that are built into our republic were intentional and meant to give us guidance and remind us that In God We Trust.

Something that I would like to point out is that a group of "old white guys," as they would be thought of today, got together about two hundred and twenty years ago and crafted a document for a totally untried form of government. They got it so right that all we have to do to save our country, even at this late date, is return to their principles, and be guided by the document that they left us. With no possible way of knowing if the government they formed would work, or what that union would face in the future, a disparate group of people came together and created a Constitution that is as close to perfect as any man made document has ever come.

Because as a Christian, I believe in free will, I doubt that the framers had "divine favor" while they were creating the Constitution. I do feel however; that the brevity and intricacy of the document coupled with the very good guidance that it has furnished (and could continue to furnish) for over two hundred years, indicates that the Founding Fathers were definitely not operating under "divine disfavor."

The nanny state built on confiscatory taxation, controlled by bureaucrats is completely at odds with Christian practices and teaching. While the liberals continually speak of "helping" the less fortunate, that help is meted out in such a way as to create dependant people and a dependant class that must either kick the "habit" or depend on the liberals for welfare. (For welfare think welfare program, aid to dependent children, food stamps, over two years of unemployment, disability payments, etc.) While it is against the law (correctly) for drug dealers to pedal their wares and create more drug addicts, the feds are constantly on the prowl for more people to "help" and turn into government dependants.

Are you having a little trouble keeping a roof over your head? Don't worry. We have a nice housing development for you. Don't like housing developments? Then how about some nice section eight housing? Don't worry we (the federal government) will pay all or most of the rent for you. Having a little trouble with groceries? We have a nice food stamp card for you. Haven't found a job? How about a welfare check to tide you over until that good job comes through? Oh, by the way, if you start making much reportable income, we will have to kick you out of the house, take away the food stamp card, and stop the welfare checks.

That's pretty much how the federal government helps people, and they claim to do it according to (at least when they are talking where they think actual Christians might hear them) Christian principles. As far as I can tell, nearly all government aid programs work against personal responsibility and a work ethic. Since these are two very big Christian principles, they are just a couple more things for liberals to dislike about Christianity, and additionally, something that needs to be erased from the American psyche.

Green Energy, Green Jobs, and Global Warming

Liberals make a lot of noise about "green energy," global warming, and something called "carbon credits." These are all feel-good issues that the left uses against us by appealing to our compassion. This is just another version of the "you have to be for this because only a nazi or someone named Hitler would be against it" strategy that they rely on so much. The reason that they use these types of attacks so often is because they work. For instance, a theme that is frequently put forward to further the left's side of the global warming debate is a picture of a polar bear (doesn't it look cute?) on a chunk of ice floating in the ocean all by itself. The implication of this is that we have melted away the polar ice and these poor bears are floating around out in the lonely cold ocean. The realty of the situation is that polar bears ride on ice or just swim around the ocean all the time. Oh, and by the way, if you get to close to a polar bear, it will eat you. As with most of what liberals do, "these inconvenient truths" are left out because they don't help the liberal agenda.

Being seen as champions for the animals and mother nature helps the liberal politicians harness groups like the Sierra Club, PETA (People for the Ethical Treatment of Animals), Greenpeace, and their ilk. I say that they harness them because that is what I think actually happens. While these organizations have agendas that they would like to pursue, what seems to really take place is that the leftist legislators appeal to them by supporting or appearing to support laws that would further the aims of these groups and then co-opt their membership. Although most of these groups feel that they get political support from some lawmakers because either the politician agrees with them, or is wary of aggravating a large number of people, I think that what mostly takes place is these same leftist politicians see a large group of people that they can control and thus reach some other goal. This is a case of a bunch of amateurs that would like to exert pressure unknowingly coming under the influence of a professional manipulator.

Cap and tax was exactly this type of proposal. Put forward by Obama and the left, it was touted as legislation that was meant to slow or stop global warming and just generally be so environmentally responsible that only the worst kind of ecological despoiler and polluter would oppose it. Environmental activists lined up behind this legislation. In reality, it was just a back door fee, or tax on businesses and consumers that use energy. Since I don't know anyone that doesn't use energy, that would mean everybody. Even the liberals couldn't spin this one enough to openly put it over on the American people, but, and this is a big but, they didn't miss by very much, and what did they do behind the scenes while this open, public, attention stealing debate had everybody's interest?

If you still think that the left is actually concerned about being environmentally friendly and that my take that they just use these issues to further whatever agenda they actually are working on is wrong, let's talk about electric cars.

Electric cars are something that the left pushes and pushes hard as one of the best things that we can do for the environment. Watching the propaganda put out by the liberals and the leftist environmentalist groups, you would probably reach the conclusion that if we would all park our gas burners and buy electric cars, all environmental issues, whether real or perceived, would be solved and most of our other problems would simply go away. Just the fact that everything that electric cars would supposedly do for us sounds too good to be true, should be a hint about whether or not they are as beneficial as we are told.

Just like most average citizens, once a month or so, I have to pay those pesky old bills. Believe it or not, one of those monthly bills is for electricity, and not just any old electricity either, but the kilowatt hours that I have used at my house. When I plug in another appliance, or run my air conditioner more, oddly enough, the bill from my electricity provider goes up. Now as the left would have you believe, electric cars don't cost anything to run because they use electricity. The problem with that is, there is no such thing as free electric power. There is indeed a fuel cost associated with electric cars, but not only is that seldom, if ever mentioned, people that push electric cars seem to actively discourage dissemination of this information.

Trying to gloss over the fact that electric cars actually do use a form of energy that has to be paid for is bad enough, but that is only the tip of the iceberg. There are a lot of dirty (pun intended) secrets about electric automobiles, and one of them that you really aren't supposed to notice is where that electricity comes from. Aside from the fact that you have to pay for electric power, it also has to be generated somewhere, which is why you have to pay for it in the first place.

Since I'm going to discuss how electricity is generated, I am going to have to admit that the left is right about one thing concerning electric cars. That one lonely thing is that if everybody converted to them, it probably would lower the amount of oil that we use. It wouldn't lower our fossil fuel usage overall, but it would probably drop the actual amount of oil that we burn. The reason that they are correct about this one item is that in the United States, most of our electricity is generated by burning coal. So if you are using an electric car, the chances are roughly seven to three that your clean energy, environmentally friendly, green, automobile is actually powered by coal. I wonder why the leftists haven't brought this detail up?

I find it hard to believe that the people who run our government, and are supposed to be looking out for our energy infrastructures don't know how we create electricity. If they are obscuring information about electric cars, how do they expect us to make informed decisions without the whole story?

The point is, they aren't after an informed electorate, and they don't really care about "the environment." This isn't a case of the liberals being well intentioned but ill informed. The information that they are glossing over or omitting is being left out on purpose. What they are concerned about is guiding us down the path they want us to follow. That well beaten trail is the one that leaves them in power, whatever that retention of power takes.

Constantly telling us how bad fossil fuels are and presenting themselves as self-proclaimed champions of the environment helps the liberals seem reasonable and well intentioned when they further regulate our energy creation capabilities and the way we use that energy. Since our economy is literally based on cheap energy, being able to regulate it gives them a huge hold on private enterprise and our culture in general.

As far as the left is concerned, global warming isn't a problem to be investigated, discussed, and solved if need be. Instead it is a ready-made sound bite type issue that hasn't been actually proved or disproved, which they can use as a way to browbeat concerned citizens into legislation and regulations that normally most people would oppose. As Obama's chief of staff Rahm Emanual said, "You don't ever want a crisis to go to waste."

Liberals present global warming as a man made environmental disaster that is caused by capitalist societies creating and using energy. And they almost always treat it as settled science. Not only do they act as if it is an unarguable fact that is cast in stone, they also (fortunately for us) happen to have the solution to the problem. Believe it or not, the solution to global warming seems to be more regulatory control of energy creation and usage in developed countries. (Tip: when a liberal says developed countries, they mean Western civilization.) Developing nations and Eastern countries like China and India must not be part of the problem because there doesn't seem to be nearly as much talk about regulating them.

Even thick headed leftists like Al Gore realize that to be able to scare and manipulate the masses with talk about global warming, they are going to have to at least pretend to believe in it. This presents a bit of a problem for them because the usual wealthy liberal has what most of the rest of us would consider an extravagant lifestyle. It could be awkward to be seen living high on the hog and using lots of energy while preaching from the climate change pulpit, except, don't forget the liberals are not constrained by having to stick to the facts, and they are some of the best marketers the world has ever seen.

Remember, this is a group that criticized Sarah Palin for being too inexperienced for the job of vice president at the exact same time that they were running Barak Hussein Obama and Joe Biden for president and vice president. Any organization that can get away with that has unbelievable salesmanship skills.

What these master marketers, with the assistance of Al Gore, came up with was something called "carbon credits." The way these carbon credits worked was, if you were going to use more energy, or as it is known, have a bigger carbon footprint than necessary, then you bought these carbon credits that supposedly balanced out your overly large "carbon footprint." What, you ask, is a carbon credit?

You will have to bear with me here, since I view carbon credits by the semi-official name that I use for them, which is somebody conning Americans for money, (S.C.A.M.). As best that I can determine, carbon credits are sold by brokers that know somebody who promises to not use much energy, or decrease their energy usage and is willing to sell you a piece of paper that says since you used a lot of energy, they won't. I know, that sounds so silly that I find it hard to believe there is actually a market for these so called credits. Would you like to know another interesting tidbit about carbon credits? Al Gore is heavily invested in them. Isn't it ironic that his lavish, energy wasting lifestyle is maintained with the help of selling carbon credits? Talk about a double standard.

The left doesn't now nor have they ever, actually cared about responsible energy usage or the environment. What they do care about is power and authority at any cost. When conservatives let themselves get mired down in a debate over the nuts and bolts of some kind of legislation that is supposed to be "eco friendly" or "green," the liberals are winning. While the conservative is trying to shape responsible legislation or accomplish something that would actually be beneficial, all the liberals care about is passing laws and regulations that give them more control. They will try to get as much authority as possible in each new law, but the most important thing is just getting passage. No matter what might actually be written in a new law, by the time it actually goes through multiple layers of bureaucrats and gets implemented, they can twist it and use it however they like. If even that doesn't work for them, there are lots of liberal judges out there that will be glad to reinterpret what is actually written, or in an extreme case, even relegislate from the bench. All a good leftist needs for this process is for something to be passed in the first place.

For those of you that haven't yet had bad experiences with government bureaucracies, and wonder why I keep referring to them as something bad, I would like to mention the Environmental Protection Agency (EPA). The EPA was created in 1970 by the Nixon Administration. Since that time it has grown into a huge bureaucracy with very broad powers. Just to drive home the point of how powerful they have become, I would say that they are probably one of the most feared government agencies, possibly, second only to the IRS in how much the average citizen is wary of them. The EPA may be one of the better known powerful bureaucracies with broad powers over citizens, but the fact is, they are just one among many.

When Obama talks about creating "green jobs," he is talking about something that doesn't even actually exist. There is no such thing as a green job. There certainly are jobs that use less energy than others, and there are probably a few limited industries that could be considered as being environmentally friendly, but a totally green job would be something like herding unicorns, or photographing chimeras, oops, cameras take energy to produce so that wouldn't be a green job. Painting them instead wouldn't work either because somebody is going to have to manufacture that paint, and come to think of it, the paint brush and the canvas too.

The point is, while building wind turbines is labeled a green job, those wind turbines are made of aluminum, steel, copper, and all kinds of other minerals that have to be mined. Surely none of those materials are being produced by strip mining? They also utilize lots of fiberglass, synthetic materials, and plastics, that are probably made from oil. Not only is a lot of energy used in producing the raw materials for the turbines, but have you ever seen the size of those things? Building components of that bulk takes a pretty big manufacturing plant with lots of workers that drive lots of steel cars running on gasoline to the plants. Then they have to be shipped to the wind farm on big trucks that probably burn some kind of that nasty old oil. It doesn't end there either, have you seen what it takes to prepare an area for wind farms? There is an incredible amount of earth moving, tree cutting, and road building done before the first turbine is erected. The equipment that it takes to get these wind farms up and running is impressive, indeed, the cranes alone are huge.

Don't get me wrong; I'm not against wind energy. I think that as we build more and more wind farms, we will learn to make them more efficiently and get more out of them. I just think that calling building wind farms "green jobs" is incorrect. They are heavy industrial jobs, and a tribute to American ingenuity and the capitalist system, but they are not "green jobs."

If the Left was really interested in green jobs, they could certainly take a look at the huge failure that the Spanish economy has become. The Spanish government has already gone down the green job path and now they know that it doesn't work and that there is no such thing as a green economy. Since the left doesn't actually care about green things anymore than they really care about electric cars, they ignore the example of the Spanish economy and press on with their agenda.

As long as we allow the liberals to shape the debate about global warming, green jobs, and the environment as actually being what all these new laws, rules, and regulations are about, conservatives, business, and the average U.S. citizen will be on the losing end.

America needs to wake up to the fact that what is actually occurring is the continual power grab by the leftists in the federal government. The fact that it is being done under the guise of "the green movement" doesn't change the reality that it is in truth an extension of federal control of our day to day lives and an invasion and limiting of our personal freedoms. And all of this is happening under the liberal's usual clarion call of "taking care of us", "for our own good".

Restricting Our Drilling

The gulf oil spill was such a golden opportunity for Obama, that if he actually believed in Christmas, he would have to send the former head of British Petroleum a nice Christmas card with a personal note of thanks.

Liberals have long despised the oil industry, and anything or anyone that is part of it. Publicly, they base this intense dislike on pollution, or wasting resources, or environmental damage, or perceived collusion on gasoline prices, or just any number of other things. Al Gore said (you remember Al, the guy that didn't invent the Internet) that he wanted to eliminate the internal combustion engine over a twenty five year period.

Many oil companies are also corporations. This makes them a trifecta of hate for liberals—an oil company, a multinational company that they can't get control of, and even worse, a corporation. Liberals despise corporations as much or maybe even a little more than they do rich people (that is rich people that aren't liberals), and that's truly saying something.

I think that they do truly hate the oil industry, but for a lot of other reasons that they have to keep to themselves. Probably one of the biggest ones is that a lot of the people that run the larger oil producers are not scared of the government flunkies that want to control them. It makes it hard to extend authority into a new area if the people you are trying to browbeat tell you to "get the hell off my property." People or organizations that will stand up to bureaucracies and the bureaucrats that run them are not going to be popular with government.

Another thing that government has got to find frustrating about the oil business is that it's not something that the government can do. Drilling holes in the ground to produce hydrocarbons takes a lot of ingenuity, extreme hard work, independent thinking and quick, spur of the moment decisions. Those are all things that are not encouraged in governmental agencies (mainly because they lead to actual results).

But you say, "The government has drilled holes for weapons testing, storage, geological information, and a host of other things." That is partially correct; they have had holes dug and continue to have holes dug, but they hire private contractors to do it. The government does exercise as much control over these contractors as possible while they are drilling for them, but the result of that is it takes a lot longer to drill holes for the federal government because of the extra oversight and "help." Remember, drilling holes in the ground is actually very hard and complicated, and an organization (the feds) that can't even design a properly working low-flush toilet, isn't the group that is going to make a complicated operation go more smoothly.

Liberals have long wanted to get control of the oil business. Despite all of the talk and pushing of alternate and green energy that the liberals do, hydrocarbons are the fuel that powers the world, and if they could get firm control of those hydrocarbons, then there would be little that they couldn't regulate as they pleased. Fortunately, up to this point in time, the people that actually own the oil companies, have been able to mostly hold the federal government off. Of course it helps that every time the government has tried to do its own drilling or producing, they have failed miserably.

Before we go further, let's define *oil company owners* a little better. When the leftists are talking about oil companies, they either want you to think of some faceless uncaring entity, or, if you want to put a human face on it, then they would like you to picture someone like Rockefeller (the original oil company founding Rockefeller, not the filthy rich liberal senator), or J. Paul Getty. Not that they were bad people, but the liberals would like you to think of the term *robber baron* when you talk about oil companies. You are not supposed to remember that a lot of oil companies are small independents where the owner or owners bet everything on the exploration that they do. They don't want you to remember that a lot (most) of the big oil companies are actually publicly owned and have potentially millions of small stockholders. After all, the retired fireman next door with oil company stock in his IRA is going to be a little hard to paint as the big boogie man oil company owner that is trying to rape the environment and personally screw you at the gas pump (that is, if it weren't for big government protecting you).

The oil business creates lots of jobs, and since they are jobs that require skills and very hard work, they are generally good paying jobs, and most of them are not unionized. That's another thing that just drives the liberals nuts.

That's why the gulf oil spill was such a win-win for the liberals in general and Obama in particular. As Machiavellian as Obama is, even he could not have possibly engineered a situation that would play so well into his hands. The gulf spill gave the oil business a very bad black eye, right when the public perception of the oil business was in the ascendancy. It looked like the area of the gulf open to drilling was about to be expanded for the first time in many years, despite liberal resistance. This would have affected the U.S. economy, and thus the citizens of the United States, positively in many ways. The net result of that increase in drilling, followed by an increase in production, would have been generally helpful for the economy, and that would make it harder for the liberals to proceed with their objectives.

Instead, Obama was able to use the spill as a reason to not only decrease the area open to drilling, but to actually ban drilling for a period of time and put all proposed offshore drilling under further review. *Further review* is government code for "We'll think about it and get back to you later, much, much, later"

The ban on drilling had so many consequences that I'm sure I'm going to miss some of them, but one of them was the fact that virtually overnight Obama eliminated tens of thousands of drilling and support jobs, mostly in the coastal states like Louisiana and Texas, where the citizens and even the state governments are often very vocally anti-Obama and pro-conservative.

Of course for every action, there is an equal and opposite reaction. Weakening the economies and eliminating jobs on the gulf coast strengthened other economies and pushed job creation somewhere else. The somewhere else that benefited was countries like Venezuela (you know, our good buddy Hugo Chavez), Saudi Arabia, (birth place of most of the 9-11 hijackers), and the other OPEC countries (more good friends of ours).

Many people fixated on how long the spill went on without Obama doing anything. That is indeed something that we should concentrate on, but most draw the conclusion that he was just inept or not very bright about how he handled the situation and that is what took so long to draw it to a conclusion.

I think that his handling of it was extremely detrimental to the United States, but masterfully orchestrated to further his true goals, which have nothing to do with what benefits the United States. One thing that resulted from the furor over why he wasn't doing anything was that all that noise hid that fact that there wasn't anything that he could have done. The federal government as powerful and far reaching as it is, has almost no real knowledge of how to cap a runaway well (the oilfield term is *blowout*) and even if they did, the equipment is extremely specialized and to my knowledge the government doesn't have any of it. I'm sure that very shortly after this situation started, some smart adviser somewhere told Obama, "Our only option is to let BP handle it." Realistically, they did have some other options; they could have kicked BP off and hired another company to handle it, or they could have kicked BP off and just watched it flow. So as you can see, the only real choice was to let BP try to cap it, which of course is what they did.

While Obama was successful in drawing attention away from the fact that he wasn't all powerful enough to just stop the leak, he did leave the impression that he could have done something about it if he had just been a little more interested. Not bad spin for somebody that we often accuse of being inexperienced, badly advised, and not very smart.

What Obama could have done was give BP and the citizens of the gulf the help that they were requesting and which was available. There were a lot of federal assets that could have actually been beneficial that did not get deployed. Other countries offered all kinds of aid with specifically built skimmer ships and the like. The governor of Louisiana practically begged for permission to build sand berms along the lowland wetlands leading into the gulf, but permission was denied. (I think this was because the feds were demanding an environmental impact statement from the EPA before permission would be given.)

None of this was done; in fact most of what the administration did was work on fastening blame on BP (which never denied that they were at fault) and talk about having their boot on the neck of BP. In fact, Obama twisted their arm to furnish a very large amount of money as restitution for economic damage, and then immediately put that money under federal control. That made good news, but what actually happened was the president of the United States directly extorted money from a public corporation without the benefit of legal representation. While BP undoubtedly had and does have obligations for recompense to damaged parties, the precedent of a sitting president directly depriving a company of billions of dollars outside of the law, scares the hell out of me. I guess the party of compassion and laws (Geneva Convention rules for terrorists) has some selective rules about where laws actually apply. Of course it's no secret that Obama likes terrorists better than he likes oil companies.

Putting the federal government in charge of money is definitely putting the fox in charge of the henhouse, but there is another serious, no doubt intended, consequence of this action. Now, when some fisherman or other individual gets money as payment for damages done by the oil spill, they won't be receiving it from BP, or the state government, they will be getting it from the federal government. This means that any hoop that the federal bureaucrats dream up will have to be jumped through and it also gives the impression that any payments received now or in the future will be largesse from the feds. Surely, you say, the minions of the federal government wouldn't use this advantageous situation to the benefit of themselves or the federal government. Well, if they don't it will be a break with everything that the federal government has been doing for many years.

So Obama and the federal government not only didn't help to contain the oil spill, they actively stood in the way of people that either could or would try to do something about it. That means that more oil is spread around the gulf than should have been. Very conveniently, all of the oil can be blamed on BP. Now when someone comes across oil in the gulf now, they are going to cuss big oil. What they aren't going to say is, "I bet that oil wouldn't be here if the federal government hadn't stood in the way of cleanup efforts." But for sure, some of the oil that will be discovered in the gulf wouldn't be there if the Obama Administration had actually wanted to be helpful.

Would it be ungracious of me to point out that all of the gulf states except Florida are red states? Not only are they red states, but now they are red states that have suffered unnecessary damage to their economies through a totally unnecessary and unreasonable drilling ban. Additionally, they have suffered much more environmental damage than they should have, which will affect their economies and the U.S economy for years to come. All of this extra environmental harm can be and should be laid directly at the feet of Barack Hussein Obama. What makes it better is that this was done solely to further his agenda. What political goal could possibly be worth this kind of human and environmental damage? I can't think of anything that could possibly be beneficial to the interests of the United States that could come out of the way the gulf oil spill was handled by Obama.

Everything that Obama did concerning the gulf oil spill was bad for us. There is no way that a president that had the best interests of the United States at heart would have acted in the way that he did. It wasn't just inaction; foreign countries that wanted to aid us were not allowed to, and state governments that wanted to help themselves were stopped. Bureaucracy slowed anybody that could have helped the situation. If you think this is the way it had to be done, look at how the president of Chile handled the situation of the trapped miners. That is how a president acts who has the interests of his country and citizens truly in his heart.

Instead Obama milked the situation for every advantage he could draw from it for his personal agenda, and he did it all under the cover of trying to be "green" and environmentally responsible when this is just another example of Obama and the liberals hijacking the green agenda for their own goals.

With all that Obama was able to get from the gulf oil spill, I imagine that his only frustration with what happened there was that he didn't think of it himself.

Earmarks

As I write this, the 2010 midterms are done, the December 2010 lame duck Congress will soon be over (at last), and maybe now the new Congress that was elected in November 2010 can get in and start to repair some of the damage that has been done to the United States over the last few years. If they are going to work on the things we elected them to take care of they are certainly going to have their work cut out for them. I hope that one of the first items that they take up is the practice of *earmarking*. The political climate right now is such that we might actually be able to drive a stake through the heart of this process once and for all.

So many people, including Barack Obama, have campaigned against earmarks that it would seem that getting rid of them would be simple, just craft a bill in the house to do away with the practice, and vote on it. You would think that this would have been done already since it has been very popular lately to run on a campaign platform that includes getting rid of this damaging practice. Unfortunately, up to this point, earmarks just haven't gone away. Even at this late date (at least at the time of this writing) nearly everything that comes out of Congress is loaded with earmarks (pork).

As it stands now, it has been left to the newly elected Congress to deal with this issue, hopefully once and for all. Since the electorate de-elected a lot of liberals partly because of this process, I think the incoming Congress is the one that should be handling it. Hopefully, they will convene, do away with earmarks, and move onto other important business.

Not to go into a bunch of unnecessary detail, but the practice of earmarking roughly means inserting spending appropriations into bills that are going up for a vote. There is more to the technical details than that, but if you think of it as attaching extra spending to a bill after the open debate portion of the law making process is over, that's probably as good a way as any to think of it. One more thing: to the best of my knowledge, it takes more than one person to get an earmark inserted into a bill. That means it's a cooperative effort by a group of people to spend tax dollars without the knowledge of the taxpayers by padding the expenses of the new law. In the world of private business, we call that collusion. In the criminal law world, I believe that it is known as conspiracy. Either way, it is not something that should be going on in the U.S. Congress.

Another huge problem with earmarks is that while the process is straightforward and well known, the actual earmarks are pretty well hidden in whatever bill it is attached to. By hidden I'm referring to the fact that the general public may hear about a bill that was passed into law, but unless somebody purposefully informs them, they will never know about the individual earmarks that were in that bill. This means that a lot of money is getting spent without citizens ever hearing about it, or having any real forum to track or comment on it. This process is costing the U.S. taxpayer a lot of money. If earmarks are really important spending that is necessary and could stand on its own merit, then why are they slipped into bills without open debate?

The shame of this is that this process exists openly, and everybody is aware of it; most agree that the practice should be stopped, the voters obviously want it gone, and yet, we still have earmarks. I guess that Pelosi's promise to "drain the swamp" must not have included getting rid of pork barrel spending.

It would be an interesting piece of information to know how many legislators in Nancy Pelosi's Congress and Harry Reid's Senate actually campaigned against earmarks. I wonder if a majority of the lawmakers under Reid and Pelosi actually told their constituents "If you send me to the House (or Senate), I'm going to do away with earmarks." I do know that Obama campaigned for president on a platform that included doing away with earmarks. Of course he also campaigned on open government, transparency, and no lobbyists in his administration, so I'm not surprised that he still likes earmarks. He also claims to…, oops sorry, sometimes I can't help myself, back to earmarks

Some of the common arguments against doing away with the process that allows earmarks are that it really isn't that much money, and sometimes a convenient earmark is just what a bill needs to get the vote of a reluctant congressman. Meaning I suppose that if our reluctant congressman could take home a little "pork" to his or her constituents, then voting for the bill that pre-earmark was not good for the country, would be okay. Hmm, I'm not sure I could get behind something that resembles a bribe, or indeed that I could be very enthused about a government official who is willing to sell off a vote and any principles they might have once possessed with it. Another part of this same thought process is that if a bill won't pass without bribing people to vote for it, that bill probably needs some more work, or maybe it shouldn't pass. I wonder how many bills that passed simply because of the earmarks (bribes) in them ended up being something detrimental to the country. I bet there are a lot of them.

What I said in the previous paragraph is nothing new, and while I like to think that I write original stuff, earmarks have been discussed so much that there is really nothing fresh to say about them. You usually only find people defending the earmark process when they have either been caught doing it, or have been spotted being the beneficiary of a nice little money filled (tax dollars) earmark. At that point, when they have their hand actually in the cookie jar, they are stuck having to try and tell us that as distasteful as earmarking might look to the uneducated public, it really is a necessary political process, and by the way, it really isn't that much money. And, don't forget, that's the way we've done it for years.

One other time that you can catch a politician defending earmarks is when they are in so much trouble at home with their constituents (think Arlen Specter) that they have to do anything they can to try and convince the local voters that despite their abysmal record, they really are representing the people at home. A dam, new highway, large school, or national park is just the kind of spending these people like to try when they need to buy a few votes at home.

Most of the time, you don't hear any of this pro-earmark language anywhere near an election. At election time, Earmarks are bad, and must be done away with. We heard a lot of talk and campaigning against earmarks in the 2010 midterms, so as I have already said, maybe this time, we can actually get rid of this corrupting process.

I have high hopes for the incoming conservatives, but remember, they are going to be taking on some very entrenched bureaucrats and Obama, so they will need our help, support, and guidance. If you don't let your congressman know what you want, then how are they going to know what you want?

In my opinion, the most common argument that politicians make for keeping the earmark process intact is that we've been doing it this way for years and as bad as it may look from the public perspective, this is just part of the legislative process.

I agree, that is the way we've done it for years and years, and look where we are now. If our present situation looks like a success, I sure don't want to see what a total screw up looks like. Earmarks aren't just a little bit of money that smoothes the operation of the Congress, they are the first drink for an alcoholic. Earmarks don't just look like a bribe; they are a bribe. They are a stumbling block on the road to recovery for our spend-a-holic federal government and they absolutely must be done away with as part of that redemption. As long as we can't muster the political and social will to do away with earmarks, not only will we not be able to regain our position of being our own masters, we won't deserve to. Getting rid of this corrupting, criminal way of stealing money from taxpayers is an absolutely necessary step in the long road back to financial responsibility and control of our out of control federal government.

As far as the statement that earmarks don't actually amount to much money, I say that in a trillion dollars, each single dollar is just as important as all the others. There is no one dollar that doesn't count quite as much as the rest of them. Not ending unnecessary, corrupting waste because theoretically, it isn't much money, is a totally nonsensical answer that is meant to distract us from the fact that there isn't any good reason to retain earmarks. Besides, if it is such a small amount of money, why are the people in Congress so unwilling to part with them? If we had done away with earmarks years ago, think how much better off we probably would be now.

While liberals argue that the actual dollar amount of the earmarks doesn't add up to a lot of money, they are only referring to the cost of the actual earmarks themselves. The way they do this, is to just go through a bill, such as the budget, and front to back, add up the actual dollar amounts of the inserted earmarks. This way, they can point at it and say that even though it might be an unpopular process, "It really isn't that much money." Oddly, this is pretty much exactly what conservative watchdog groups do so that they can point at the same figures and say, "Look how much earmarks cost."

While I think I've made pretty clear that I think the whole earmark process is corrupt, immoral, and should be prosecutable, I vehemently disagree with the way the cost of earmarking is tallied.

Adding up the total earmarks in a spending bill and saying that is the price tag of earmarking is not even touching the surface of what this practice has and continues to cost us. How many spending bills have passed only because they contained earmarks? Way too many. How much bad law that costs us money and will continue to cost us money has made it through Congress because of bribes (earmarks)? Can you say health care? Earmarks helped pass a twenty seven HUNDRED page health care bill after the average American taxpayer made it perfectly clear they didn't want that particular bill passed. Are you starting to get the idea that earmarks are a really bad practice that our parents should have stopped years ago?

The fact of the matter is that one result of earmarks is a lot of bad bills being passed. The liberals know this; it is one of their primary ways of getting conservatives to "reach across the aisle." This way they get the double benefit of passage of parts of the liberal agenda, and additionally a little "ownership" of the people that succumb to the temptation of earmarks.

The cost of the passage of unknown numbers of bad bills that wouldn't have made it without earmarks is incalculable. Some of these programs have been with us for decades, and will continue on for decades more. How much unnecessary spending do we have to support annually because of earmarks?

If we do away with earmarks, I bet we will find that a lot fewer bills get passed. I also think that what does get through after earmarks are abolished will have a much better chance of actually being beneficial to our society. I wonder what bill the funding for crucifixes in jars of urine has been hiding in? I also wonder how well that funding would do in an open debate on the floor of the house.

If our parents and grandparents had stopped earmarking many years ago, we could potentially be much better off today. However; our parents didn't take care of this issue, so now it is up to us. We have a duty to represent present taxpayers (ourselves) and future taxpayers (our children and grandchildren) and get this practice stopped. It will be generational crime to let this wasteful practice burden our descendants one bit more than it already has. It is our patriotic duty to urge our politicians to get rid of this despicable practice, and start us on the road to financial responsibility.

The conservatives that we elected in November ran on openness, integrity, and conservative values. What better way for them to start off in 2011 than a bill from the House to do away with earmarks? Now is the time to start getting control of the spending that is being done by the monster the federal government has become, and I think people will be surprised by how large the amount of spending that results from the earmarking process is.

Even if a bill to stop earmarks fails, at least the American public will be able to see who voted against it. Hiding wasteful spending behind the scenes has got to stop and an open vote on a bill to remove earmarks from the political process should show who is and who isn't for it quite nicely.

I think the United States of America is the best country that has ever existed in the world. I also think that we can do better in the future, but to do that, we are going to have to get our spending under control, and one good first step in that process is to do away with earmarks.

Illegal Immigration

One of the bigger issues that is a clear example of what's going on between the conservatives and the liberals right now is the continuation of illegal immigration and the status of the illegal immigrants that are already here. On one side the big spending pro-government control leftists don't care at all what actually happens to the illegal immigrants but see a good opportunity to use another group of people that has become available for exploitation to further their aims. On the other side, the conservatives want to do something to solve this problem in as humane and equitable of a manner as possible.

For the left, illegal immigration has everything; the liberals want to allow it to continue and additionally grant amnesty and full citizenship to any and all illegal immigrants that they can. These people are tailor made for the left; they are undereducated, poor, easily influenced with a few government handouts, and since many of them are already used to living in squalor and poverty, they will fit right in to the entitlement programs and housing that the left can't wait to give them. If only the nasty old conservatives would just get out of the way, there will be millions of new voters ready to toe the line for the liberal politicians. So as you can imagine, the left throws the word *racist* around a lot when they are trying to push something through on this issue.

Just to point out again what master manipulators the liberals are, they intend to treat these potential new, mostly Hispanic, voters just like they have treated the blacks and other poor people that they have supposedly helped out over the years, and yet the Hispanic groups strongly support the liberals. The liberals don't even try to hide what's in store for these people. They (leftists) are very up front about wanting to enroll them into the same programs that they are using to "help" the poor people that are on the federal dole now. Since that "help" has just about destroyed the very people that are supposedly being "helped", if I were a group of Hispanics, I think that I would try to negotiate a better deal than what they are being offered.

So at first look, this is a debate between two groups that are arguing over whether or not we are going to put a stop to it and if or when we do, what we will do with the illegal immigrants that are already here. The left has very cleverly guided the debate so that it is very narrowly limited to arguing about whether or not they (the immigrants) are watering down public services, such as schools and hospitals, and whether or not they are a drain on the tax base, or actually net contributors to the tax base because of their supposed inability to withdraw tax dollars that they pay in.

You would think that debating on these points would work against the left because we could actually dig up some facts and present real figures to settle these arguments, at last backing the liberals down with reality and logic. This of course is where the liberals start bringing out emotional arguments and comparing conservatives to Hitler, then as soon as that is over, out comes the race card.

What's so clever about all of this is that other than the potential for more liberal voters, the real use of the illegal immigrants for the left is to water down the economy. Illegal immigrants aren't here to do jobs that Americans won't do; that is a fiction shouted so long and so often by liberals and Hispanic groups that people have actually started to believe it. What illegal immigrants are doing is working in harsh conditions and for low wages that Americans can't work under because the liberals have made it against the law. You certainly could find Americans who would work for less than seven dollars an hour, but since the liberals keep raising the legal minimum wage, the left has literally outlawed any American citizen, whatever their race, from taking that job. Not only have they outlawed lower wages for citizens, they have heaped so many fees, taxes, and regulatory control on businesses that legitimately hire legal citizens, that they are monetarily discouraging the hiring of Americans and encouraging the utilization of off the books illegal labor.

So the illegal immigrants are a potential future block of new federal dependants that can certainly be trained to vote for the hand that feeds them. How many generations of federal dependency do you think it will take to get rid of their work ethic? Even if that doesn't happen, or at least until it does, they are very handy to the left as a tool to keep the lower economic classes of legal citizens from finding a starting place at the bottom of the jobs ladder and working themselves up into the middle class. This also has the dual effect of shackling the growth of the small businesses that have to start off using unskilled labor. You know, the very entities that our economy depends on for growth and job creation. The liberals talk about job growth, but that's all hot air; what they really do, and illegal immigration is only one example of it, is to talk about starting the engine of economic growth but firmly set the parking brake instead.

Since a thriving, vigorous private sector usually resents extra government intrusion and regulation, the goal of the left has never been to do what is actually good for small businesses and job creation. Not that they mind a good economy, as long as they can stay in power, but good economies happen in spite of the liberals, not because of them. The actual goal is control, or power over of as much of the public and private sector that they can get. The problem of illegal immigration is just one more thing that liberal politicians have purposefully let build up into a huge festering mountain of trouble and human misery that must be solved by, you guessed it, more intervention by the federal government and more huge entitlement programs that need to be staffed by, hang on, more bureaucrats.

If the left was actually interested in doing something about illegal immigration, they would not have attacked Arizona over the recent attempt by that state to have the actual federal immigration laws enforced. Instead the federal government had to have Arizona's attempt struck down for two reasons. One, it probably would have worked and stopped a large number of the illegal immigrants that come into, and already are in Arizona. Two, and this is why the state's attempt was doomed from the outset, the federal government cannot have any particular state stand up to the feds, win, and be an example to other states. Something like this could lead to "gasp," the states actually holding the feds' feet to the fire and having them live up to the real obligations of the federal government. Remember, we aren't talking about a state trying to secede from the union; we are talking about a state that desperately wants the federal government to enforce the federal laws, nothing more and nothing less than that.

To put it in perspective, what if the liberal federal government decided that those pesky old restrictions on the imminent domain laws were getting in the way, so they just stopped enforcing them in your states? Oops, sorry. I forgot, they already did that. Darn it, I hope my state government can stand up for me here in case some developer decides that they like the land my house sits on. Oh, shoot, we just saw how effective it was for Arizona to try to stand up to the feds. Uh oh, I really hope one of Barney Frank's buddies doesn't need some land for a new shopping center.

Do you see why the federal government striking down Arizona's attempt to enforce the federal law is both so important, and also so much more than just a minor scuffle over illegal immigrants? The left very cleverly kept the focus of this fight between Arizona and the federal government centered on immigrants. This way they turned it into another argument where they could try to claim the high moral ground because after all, "We are just talking about poor, underprivileged people who only want to work."

The dispute between Arizona and the feds wasn't about illegal immigrants. It was about a state desperate for the federal government to stand up to its obligations and laws. You would never know that from what the main stream media ran on the subject. If you took what the leftist media said to heart, then you would know beyond a shadow of a doubt that Arizona is filled with the most despicable, racist, lily white, future KKK recruits that ever managed to gather together long enough to elect one of their own as governor.

And let's not forget, while so called "sanctuary cities" may or may not be breaking the state laws of whatever states they are in (and they probably they are defying their own city ordinances), the major laws that they are breaking are federal immigration laws. I understand that there are almost certainly some new black panthers in some of these sanctuary cities. The presence of the new black panthers of course means that Eric Holder will be unable to lead any charge into these places to round up both the illegal aliens and the people that are harboring them in direct defiance of federal law. I also know that Janet Napolitano is busy overseeing the sexual assault of airline passengers, so she has no time to deal with sanctuary cities either, but can't we at least pull Janet (Rambo) Reno out of retirement to deal with them? She could grab a few tanks, a bunch of machine guns, dust off her plans for the invasion of the Branch Davidian compound and her snatching of Elian Gonzalez then go straight to work. Just tell her that there are children in there that need to be separated from their parents and watch that girl go (Doesn't the liberal compassion that's just oozing from her agent in the picture where he is holding Elian Gonzalez at gunpoint just warm the cockles of your heart). She can use that same liberal compassion that she demonstrated in the two incidents that I named and after one or two invasions of sanctuary cities, I expect we would have a mass surrender.

By the way, I would like to remind everybody that the new black panthers that Eric Holder isn't prosecuting were violating federal laws by intimidating voters at a polling place where a national election was being held. Hmm, but these new black panthers were intimidating people that they thought were going to vote against Obama. Surely, there isn't any tacit approval from the administration for this. I sure hope that partisan, billy club wielding, election supervisors isn't the fundamental change that we were promised. I mean that would be like, um, I don't know, uh, oh, I know, a good example would be like holding a workplace election deciding whether or not to unionize, but instead of the normal way we vote (secret ballot), having all the votes recorded by name. You know something that would be called card check. Uh,oh, this is looking bad, but maybe the state government could step in and save us, whoops.

This is all coming to a head under Obama; if you still think that I am wrong, and Obama isn't really trying to harm the United States, how do you explain a federal government that absolutely refuses to enforce its own laws against illegal immigration and voter intimidation and makes sure that nobody else does either? Do you think that Eric Holder, the attorney general, could decide on his own not to prosecute the new black panthers?

One more dirty little detail about illegal immigration and this is one that the left really won't like, but here we go: the problem can be solved. There, was that so hard to say? I know that the left constantly preaches that this is an unsolvable issue, but if you pay attention, they say that about everything. Their goal is to convince you, me, and everybody else that problems are too big to be solved, and the only thing that will come close to (but oddly, never quite actually solve) handling our big problems is federal intervention and supervision, and lots of it. This is what these power hungry, soul sucking, leftists do for a living. If we were to start resolving issues, then they would not only be out of power, but might even have to do some kind of real work. Now that's a thought that would definitely get a liberal out speaking in favor of unemployment extensions.

Do I know what the exact, best solution of the illegal immigration issue is? No, of course not. Do I think that it will be simple and easy? No, I think it will require some pretty tough decisions, but I think it will be a lot easier to do than the liberals would have us believe. Remember, this is the United States of America, the greatest country that has ever existed on the face of the earth. All we need to do to solve our problems, and illegal immigration is one of them, is recognize the problem, decide that we are going to face it head on, and then do it.

State and Municipal Governments

So if I've spent so much ink in this book trashing the federal government and liberals, why have I left the state and municipal governments alone? Have I perhaps decided that only the federal government is rife with power hungry politicians?

First of all, for the purposes of this discussion, I'm going to lump all forms of government that aren't the federal government into the categories of state and municipal government. Before I go on, I would like to point out that there are a lot of governing bodies that we utilize in the United States. They include, but are by no means limited to county (or parish), city, hospital districts, water districts, transportation districts, emergency service (such as rural fire, ambulance, or etc) districts, school boards, and basically any board, council, or other form of administration that has the power to levy taxes, oversee disbursement of tax payer funds, or provide a public service at taxpayer expense.

As I said, there are a lot of different governing bodies that each individual citizen of the United States is subject to. Most of these bodies are prone to having some of the same problems and abuses as the federal government, and when they do, the difference is mainly a matter of scale. To put it bluntly, a dishonest state politician can't steal as much as a crooked federal politician because there just isn't as much money floating around at the state level as there is at the federal level. Additionally, bad state laws aren't going to affect as many people as a bad federal law because they only apply to one state, not fifty of them. This decrease in effect magnifies as you go down the chain to the smaller municipal governments. Admittedly, the city governments of someplace like New York City, Houston Texas, and Los Angeles California, are going to affect several million people, but at the end of the day, they are still just city governments.

While there is no doubt in my mind that you can find shady politicians in any form of government no matter how big or small, I do think that the smaller forms of government right up to the state level are where you are going to find some elected officials that are there because of something they believe in. These are the people who feel so strongly about an issue or issues that they have decided to take personal action and have run for the office that they can use to deal with those issues. These are the citizen legislators that we would like to have instead of career politicians. At least that's how a lot of them start out. Some are "captured" by the system and then become career politicians. By the way, I think this capture is much more common at the federal level than any other. A lot of municipal governments only pay a nominal one dollar a year or no salary at all. A job with no pay is not a lot of incentive for an honest person to become a career politician. Notice that I specified an *honest* politician.

The main reason that I have concentrated on the federal government instead of the state or municipal governments isn't because I think that state and local entities don't need oversight and improvement. The reason that I have a lot less of a problem with the smaller forms of government is precisely because they are smaller and even at the state level, basically local entities.

The main problem with the federal government right now is that it is has reached the point that the unchecked liberalism of that federal government in the hands of a relatively small amount of greedy, unscrupulous people has actually become an entity that under Obama is about to destroy us. At a time like this, having stronger state governments than we do would definitely be helpful. Instead, we have a few states that are trying to stand up to the federal government, but these states are in the minority, and they are also fighting a very uphill battle.

If you live in one of the states that are presently defying the federal government by taking the struggle for your rights to the federal courts, you should support your state government in that endeavor. The states that are trying to contain the intrusion of the federal government are doing exactly what they are supposed to, and that is fighting for their residents. Any victory whether large or small, that rolls back the powers that the federal has usurped is a plus. I do suppose it's possible that there are people out there that don't think the states should be trying to stand up to the federal government, but I doubt that any of them are reading this book.

If the government of a state is totally out of control, or just doing something extremely unpopular on one issue, whatever the problem is, that is an item that the state's citizens can and should take up with their government. It is quite possible for the citizen of an individual state to make his or her opinion known to every one of their state's representatives up to and including the governor or at least the governor's office. Quite often, it is actually doable to just go knock on a door or make a phone call and talk directly to a state representative. Any time that you can have contact at that kind of personal level, whatever you are dealing with is a local issue.

I'm often at functions where my state representative is present. I could certainly talk to her then if I like, or if I needed more of her time than a word in passing, I could call her office and make an appointment. (I do say hello when I see her, but as I generally agree with her ethics, I don't waste her time trying to supply her with the minutiae of my political thinking.) I live in the second most populous state in the United States, and if I can have this kind of personal contact with my state representatives, how much easier must it be in smaller or small states?

If, in your opinion, the local school board has just gone nuts, then it is quite possible to just run for the school board yourself and see if you can make the changes that are dear to your heart. Of course, I would advise that you look into the matter closely before you run; it's likely that what concerns you the most about your schools is actually something that is mandated by the state or federal government and the school board is just complying with an existing law that they had no part in creating.

One important thing that I would like to point out about state and local governments is that since they are very much more open to contact with and participation by the citizens, it is your civic duty to supply that contact and participation. If you don't like the way your local government boards are performing, at the very least, make your opinions known. If you do like the way they are carrying out their functions, they need to know that too.

Many state and local boards such as zoning committees and tax appraisal boards are made up of volunteers. If you think you can do a better job, then volunteer for that work and do a better job. If you are an independent businessman and don't like the way your city treats existing businesses, there are all kinds of civic organization both inside and outside of government that deal with this issue and a host of others. Become involved, put your experience and time to good use in our citizen government. Don't say you can't find the time, because if nobody finds the time to fill these spots and address these vital issues, then you will later have to find the time to deal with unpleasant issues such as higher taxes, unnecessary or detrimental rules and regulations, along with runaway, uncontrollable government.

If you think inattention to small local governments and the larger state governments won't result in the problems that I've pointed out, take another look at the federal government that we've been talking about for this whole book. The federal government started off as a small, citizen friendly government and look where it is now.

Another way that state and local governments can be dealt with that usually isn't a practical way for the average American to deal with the federal government is voting with your feet. If there is something going on with the state, county, city, or other municipal district that you live in that has just flat become intolerable to you, the option always exists to move to another area that is more to your liking. Granted, although it does happen, it isn't all that common for people to sell their houses and move to another area only because of some governmental issue. What does happen very frequently is that people look very closely at the government institutions such as water districts, county, city, and school boards that have jurisdiction in the area they are thinking about moving into.

What is more likely to happen to an abusive local government entity is that over time people move away when an economic opportunity to do so becomes available. That steady drain of population coupled with a lower number of new people moving in will economically affect the region. This type of thing can be on a very small scale, such as different sections of a city that are known to have poor local schools, or it can happen on a much larger, state sized level.

A really good example that is happening right now is the difference between Illinois and Texas. Both states are experiencing significant budget shortfalls. In the case of Illinois, what they have done is raise their state taxes over 60 percent. That is an amount that I definitely consider to be abusive, but I don't live in Illinois and my only response to what is a problem for the citizens of that state, is to be glad that I'm not one of them. Of course, when I hear that it is Illinois, and I see the politicians that they have been producing lately, I'm not surprised that their answer to any kind of government spending problem is to increase taxes. I would expect nothing else. However, no matter what my opinion of how the state of Illinois handles itself is, the governance of that entity is a matter between the Illinois state government and its citizens.

The Texas government on the other hand has vowed to cut spending instead of raising taxes. Is the process of cutting spending going to cause some problems? Yes, I'm sure that some things that should be funded will be eliminated or cut, and I'm equally sure that some things that should have been done away with long ago will continue to exist in the Texas government. The point is however, that those are local issues that the citizens of Texas can hash out with their own state government, and they will do that from a position of not having their taxes abusively raised.

As things stand right now, between Illinois and Texas, which state do you think is going to gain taxpayers, and which state is going to start losing their taxpaying population? A shift like this is going to really hit Illinois hard, because the only citizens that are going to be incentivized to move out of Illinois are going to be the taxpayers. If you aren't actually paying taxes, then a tax increase isn't going to bother you nearly as much as it does the people "toting the freight." Illinois citizens that are receiving some kind of public assistance to live on aren't going to worry very much about a tax increase as long as that public assistance continues. So what Illinois and other entities that take the path of huge tax increases are doing is urging the people that actually create the revenue, to leave.

While quickly moving in and out of areas as different governing bodies implement unfavorable laws or restrictions is not an option that is easily available to private citizens, it is an option that often is available to businesses.

One of the leftist's biggest complaints, among many, about large corporations is that a lot of them have moved out of the United States or moved significant portions of their operations overseas to avoid taxes here. This is nothing more than a result of the high taxes and other abuses that the left heaps on corporations. Businesses must go where they can make profit, so if we overtax or restrict them in other unnecessary ways, they are going to move to a place where they can do business more profitably. And before you say "that's a pretty mercenary way to do business," remember that if you own stock in a large corporation that is not returning profit on your investment, you will probably either complain or sell that stock and buy some in a company that will make a profit for you. There's nothing mercenary about it; businesses are morally bound to make a profit for their owners.

This same relocation of business happens on a smaller scale between the different states. When it becomes more profitable for a business to relocate to another state, at some point they will do just that. Another thing that business looks at before deciding on a state to do business in is the number and quality of the workforce. States that are bleeding taxpayers (workers) are not good candidates for a business to move into and states with poor education systems are also not places that pick up a lot of new businesses.

In short, the only difference between the possible abuses at the state and local level versus the federal level is a difference in scale. Most of the smaller governing bodies are subject to the same types of issues that we are dealing with in the federal government. The difference is, at the state and local levels; we can and do deal with government problems in a local manner.

This option does not exist at the federal level. The federal government is too large, too far away, and too spread out to be dealt with by individual citizens. We must depend on our elected officials to that government to oversee the proper day to day and year to year functioning of that national government.

As I write this book, that's not happening.

Will Stopping and Getting Rid of Obama Solve All Our Problems?

Although the most immediate problem that faces us right now is Barack Hussein Obama, he is not ultimately our biggest problem, just the most pressing one. Even if we were to somehow negate his influence from this point forward that alone, is not going to solve our difficulties. Unfortunately, Obama himself has already done so much harm that if we were to stop him now, what has already happened up to this point is going to be very tough to deal with and undo. The large debt above and beyond what we had already foolishly accumulated is going to take real effort by serious people who are truly trying to salvage our republic and the American dream.

There is no doubt in my mind that Barack Obama has done the harmful things that he has done to our country on purpose. I feel that he is probably the best political manipulator the world has ever seen. He manages to wring political advantage for his goals out of nearly every situation that comes up on so many different levels at the same time that I can only watch in stupefied amazement and wonder how much good he could have done for this country and the world if he was actually a patriotic American that truly wanted to serve the best interests of the United States of America.

Watching how he manipulated the events of a sudden, totally unexpected catastrophe like the gulf oil spill and with no prior notice or any time to plan still manage to turn everything about that disaster to his complete advantage was a real eye opener. Not only that, remember he accomplished that feat and everything else he has done right out in broad daylight.

This is the part where I remind you that even this far down the line, if you still do not believe that Obama is purposefully damaging the United States, it really doesn't matter whether he is doing what he is doing intentionally or not. Even if Obama is merely a political buffoon of legendary proportions, who bumbles from one disaster to another, accidentally causing horrendous damage everywhere he goes, whether done accidentally or on purpose, the effect of the damage is the same.

Still, even with everything that he has accomplished (toward his goals), bad intent or not, it would seem fairly simple for our lawmakers to just reverse what has happened. They could defund his programs, deprive the White House of extra money, repeal things like health care, tie his numerous czars and advisers up in hearings, and just generally bring the executive branch to a stop. Unfortunately, that would depend on Congress to "coming to its senses."

Have you taken a close look at Congress lately? Harry Reid, Nancy Pelosi, and their ilk are still there. The 2010 midterm elections were a good start, but one election no matter how successful for honest politicians is not even a good start on house cleaning. Before you say, "Hey, you didn't mention that tying up the executive branch like that would also encumber Congress to the point where they wouldn't be able to get much done either." I thought about that. With the large number of leftists that are still in Congress, I figure that keeping them occupied with something other than passing legislation will probably work out okay.

The reason that Barack Hussein Obama was able to gain control of the huge federal bureaucracy and pass wildly inappropriate laws is precisely because of the lawmakers that exist and did exist in Congress. I honestly have not been able to figure out the motivation of people like Harry Reid and Nancy Pelosi, but whatever drives those two people, it isn't good for our country. Additionally, super skilled political manipulator or not, Obama could not have ripped into our society and institutions with the effect that he has without those two specifically and others of their type (can you say Barney Frank?) that are not as well known.

As I have repeatedly brought up throughout this book, as bad as Obama has been for this country, he would not have been able to seize the reins of a well run healthy republic and kick it into high gear to start tearing it apart. All of the things that he has done are just built on means and methods that already existed. One good example is the bribery that went into passing health care. Openly offering senators and representatives fat, juicy incentives to pass the health care bill that they normally would have voted against would not have been acceptable if it weren't for the fact that earmarks exist. Since we are already in the habit of allowing our congressional politicians to bribe each other through the earmark process, it just doesn't seem like a big deal when Pelosi and Reid openly offer large money incentives for particular holdouts in Congress.

This is the legacy of the earmarking process. Remember when I said that the cost of earmarks is probably incalculable? Well, the loss of integrity in our political representatives due to the open acceptance of earmarks, potentially has cost us several TRILLION dollars in the ONE instance of passage of the healthcare law. Do you still think that earmarks are something that doesn't actually add up to much money?

When pork addicted politicians are trying to tell you that earmarks are not that big a deal because they don't really add up to a lot of money, and by the way, that is just the way we have always done business, just think of them as unrepentant spend-a-holics that aren't willing to give up their addiction to your money. These people very obviously existed before Obama came and nothing other than the 2010 midterm elections has been done to stop them and their spending habits.

These power and money-addicted politicians are the same crowd that (at the time of this writing) are out there preaching long and loud that we absolutely must raise the debt ceiling and borrow more money than ever before, again. Right now, no room is being given for just cutting federal budget and reducing spending. As soon as spending reduction is brought up, out comes the threat that "we'll have to shut down the government."

What the solution to the present, so called "budget crisis" will be, I have no way of knowing at this time. While I personally hope that a lot of useless or even harmful federal programs are greatly reduced or eliminated, I know that if that is indeed what happens, it will be after a lot of struggle and rhetoric in the press and the Congress. Dire consequences will be threatened by the left at every turn, predictions of economic chaos and societal harm will be a dime a dozen, and of course, the conservatives will be cast as hard hearted nazi-like uncaring racists. This is just business as usual for the left, and since their most treasured institution, federal bureaucracies, will be threatened, I expect the volume and frequency to be impressive.

So even if Obama was to be negated right now, we are still going to be stuck with the leftist policies and the liberals that create and maintain them. Even worse, now those same big spenders have had a taste of government control and spending on a scale that they never dreamt of in their most ambitious daydreams.

I think the spending and other policies that Obama has created and pushed through are to big spending federal politicians as gasoline is to a fire. When we start trying to undo the damage of the last two years, we are going to find that the left, even without Obama's influence, is going to be very attached to the new level of spending. I feel sure that at least to start with, it will seem like battling the mythical hydra, where when you cut off one head, two more grow in its place.

Does anybody out there think that even if Obama is thwarted in his programs now, that the federal fingers he has extended into large industry and banking are just going to disappear overnight? Right now, we have a "czar" who is in charge of deciding whether the CEOs of the companies that are beholden to the federal government are being paid properly or not. That means that when these chief executive officers are dealing with the federal government, they are talking to the people with control over their personal paycheck. Doesn't that make you wonder how hard these people are going to argue about federal policies that are harmful for their companies, and also how effective they can be at trying to get the federal government out of their companies business? This control of CEO pay was just a very clever way for Obama and his minions to skirt the laws and get some control of large businesses without having to bother with pesky things like the legality of what they were doing.

Does anybody out there really believe that the leftist politicians are going to willingly surrender a sweet method of getting in the back door of the corporate boardroom like that one? I think we are going to have a hard time rolling something like this back, and while we are doing it we will be subjugated to a barrage of hype from the media and the left about being in the pocket of big business.

Ridding ourselves of Obama will not erase the leftist policies that existed before him; in fact we will be hard pressed to just get back to the state of overspending and borrowing that existed before his election. However, difficult or not, we must get control of the massive bureaucracy that used to be a government and tame the abuse and misuse of that beast. As I've already mentioned, Obama didn't create anything that wasn't already there; he merely used what existed before he was elected, and the problems that we should have been dealing with long before Obama came along are still there and are still waiting for us to fix them.

Another issue that didn't originate with Obama, that has caused problems in the past and will cause more in the future, is the liberal bias in the media. Since I believe very firmly that a free press is absolutely essential to a free citizenry, I have no suggestions on how to "deal" with the liberal media. The leftist bias is a problem that has plagued the United States for years, but my only proposal for handling it is better education for our children so that they are able to sort through the bias and make informed decisions. I suspect that if we can deal successfully with our other big problems, of which declining education is one, then the liberal bias in the media will probably be self correcting. I do think that any attempt to regulate the media, such as the "fairness" doctrine is a very bad idea and should not ever be done by either side.

Repealing Obama care will not automatically undo the damage that has been done to our health care system. There have already been a lot of medical professionals who have either retired or are now planning to retire early, and I am sure there have also been a lot of promising young people that have decided to not enter the medical field because of what they see coming from government controlled health care.

Talk about the liberal media bias, I saw a report on ABC.com that listed the statement that Obama care is a government takeover of the health care system as the biggest political lie of 2010. If Obama care isn't the government takeover of the American health care system, as far as I'm concerned, it will do until the real thing comes along.

I personally don't think that our health care system was "broken" or even damaged before Obama got his hands on it. I'm convinced that the high costs of our health care have a lot more to do with government interference in the insurance business and medical profession coupled with a decided lack of tort reform than any supposed "predatory" practices by health care professionals. Since I don't think the system was broken, a return to where we were a few years ago, accompanied with a hard, conservative, businesslike look into what is really driving health costs up would probably solve this overblown (by the left) non-problem. I do think that anything we do concerning health care should start with an apology to every person in the health care field in general and all doctors in particular for all of the abusive statements that have been made about them and the health care profession by Obama, his cronies, and the leftists for the last few years.

Barack Hussein Obama did not invent the leftist agenda, he did not start us on a creeping path to European style socialism, he did not create the liberal bias that exists in our supposed to be impartial press, he did not create massive federal entitlement programs, he did not develop the partisan debate tactics of the leftists, he did not start the denigration of the American capitalist system. I could go on and on about the things the left has created, invented, and utilized that Barack Obama didn't invent or foster. The point is, all of the things I've listed and much more are part of the lefts agenda, and while Obama didn't create them, he has definitely put them to use as part of his personal agenda, whatever that might be.

Just as he (Obama) didn't dream these things up, they, unfortunately, won't go away when he does. These are all issues that should have been dealt with before, and since they won't leave with Obama, just stopping him isn't going to do what we as a country should have done a long time ago, which is face these issues head on and solve them, not continue to put them off for later generations as has been the practice in the past.

What Obama has done, is bring all of our political and social issues to the forefront. It would be sweet irony indeed if Obama's attempt to ruin us ends up being the very thing that finally gets our attention and results in a political pulling together to grasp the opportunity to bring our country back to the republic that our Founding Fathers left us.

The only thing that stands between us and that goal is the decision to do it and the resolve to carry it through. The time is now, the place is here, which side are you on?

Solutions

So other than generally saying, "We need to become more involved in our government," what are some real solutions to our problems?

First, do indeed become more involved in our government; this is one place where the left beats out the conservatives nearly every time. Since for the most part liberals enact legislation that has something in it for themselves or their voting bloc, they are usually able to generate a lot of interest. On the other hand, the left usually portrays anything that conservatives are doing as harmful to entitlements, so that also generates a lot of bad press for conservative agendas. When the liberals are being vocal about putting more federal regulations and laws in place, conservatives need to be just as noticeable and as aggressive with their views. If you think the fairness doctrine is a bad idea (as any intelligent person would), then the next time the left brings it, or any other harmful program up, don't just make your opinion known, make it very well known.

Becoming more involved in our own government means a lot more than just reading articles and voting on Election Day. It means finding out what your government is up to and then letting your representatives know where you stand. This includes all levels of government from the smallest town council all the way through the county, state, and national governments. If you don't take the time to let them know what you think, then they will be ignorant of your opinion, and also at the same time, it will seem that you are indifferent to how they go about taking care of the business of government that they are elected to. Staying in touch with your representatives does more than just let them know what's on your mind; it also reminds them that they are being watched. Even the worst of the pork barreling, vote selling crowd will be much more careful about how they operate if they know that their constituents are paying attention to how they vote and what they support.

Most of the bad things that have happened to us are a direct result of the general public not paying attention to anything but the biggest issues, and sometimes not even giving that little bit of consideration to current events. After all, the federal deficit, budget amounts, and tax rates are talked about every year, but until now, when they have become a must solve problem, we, the taxpayers and voters, have not really done anything about them. In this regard, we have ourselves to blame for how far this situation has deteriorated. Fortunately, with a change in attitude, we also can look to ourselves for the solution to these problems.

Secondly, we must again become a nation of laws. We need to return to constitutional law and those laws must be enforced fairly and impartially as they were meant to be. What we have now is a tangle of laws and regulations, many of which are of dubious constitutionality at best, that are enforced or not enforced as the people in charge decide. Not only is this not a workable system, it also leads to extensive abuse and favoritism; in fact, that's exactly why the entities or individuals that don't enforce or even worse, selectively enforce laws, do it.

What's the difference between non-enforcement and selective enforcement? The way I would define non-enforcement would be when an authority, or governing institution just determined that they didn't like a particular regulation and decided that that law would not be enforced in their jurisdiction. Something like the sanctuary cities that refuse to enforce the immigration laws. In fact, agencies of the federal government often do not enforce federal law. An example of this would be the laws against felons or other people that are prohibited by law from attempting to buy guns. As far as I am aware, when these people are found out by a background check, all that happens to them is they are not allowed to complete the purchase of the weapon.

As bad as it is for the rule of law in the United States to not enforce the laws of the land (and as far as I'm concerned, Obama is encouraging this), even worse are laws that are selectively enforced. Selective enforcement would be things like, oh, I know some, finding out that someone had a drunken wreck that resulted in a young woman drowning and not even attempting to prosecute the driver for the drowning; catching someone lying under oath but then not prosecuting them for perjury; or, and I know this is a stretch, how about someone having a gay prostitution ring being run out of his house but not prosecuting the person because he claimed not to have known anything about it? As you can see, there are a lot of people running around out there who could probably be classified as unindicted criminals. This is all due to selective enforcement of our laws.

I hope none of these people have ever been involved in our government or have never had anything to do with writing laws or guiding policy. That sure would be bad for us. I mean after all, we wouldn't want anybody who thought it was okay to leave a woman to drown or somebody that was okay with prostitution rings to have been handling the reins of our government, would we?

Stopping the habitual selective enforcement or non-enforcement of our laws must be part of the return to even handed rule of law that we are quickly leaving behind. It will do us no good to deal with our financial problems if this issue is not addressed.

Since the problems that face our republic are numerous and varied, the solutions we will need to solve them will have to be just as flexible. We will need decisive, ethical, patriotic politicians to sort this mess out. I don't have the answers to all the situations that we are faced with, and additionally, I don't have the perfect solution of how to get the best people available as our members of Congress, but I do have one suggestion that I think will help a lot.

I think that the single most important thing that we can do at the federal level to improve our government and thus advance our whole country is something that is so different from the usual thinking that while there are people who have suggested it, very few are willing to publicly be associated with what I'm about to propose. Kind of like the various fair tax proposals or reforming social security, there are a few people here and there that will talk about it, but when a serious show of support is called for, the silence is deafening.

What I think we should do is pay our federal senators and representatives better, and I don't mean a little better, I mean a lot better. As desirable and good for this country as it would be if all our federal lawmakers were the kind of citizen legislators that we would like to have (kind of like the character played by Jimmy Stewart in *Mr. Smith Goes to*

Washington), I think something we have pretty much proven by now is that we are never going to rid ourselves of professional politicians, and term limits are something that it is nice to talk about but realistically are never going to happen.

The fact that some kind of term limits (other than on the presidency) hasn't been instituted is not all because politicians are reluctant to instate them. A lot of it actually can be laid at our own feet, that is the feet of the taxpayers and voters. How many times have we all gone to vote, thinking that we should just turn out all the career politicians and start over? That is except for our own representative or senator that is doing an okay job. There's nothing wrong or unusual with this view; after all, as bad as rampant incumbency can be, it would be foolish to turn out a politician who really is doing a good job of looking out for their constituents and the country at the same time. Of course, then we get down to the question of whether they are actually looking out for the country or just bringing home a lot of pork to the people that can keep them in office or turn them out instead. Robert (Ku Klux Klan) Byrd should be the poster child for pork barreling, vote buying, bureaucracy growing, leftist politicians, he stayed in office for years, and in my opinion the amount of pork that he spread around to do that has greatly harmed the country.

Just a quick point that I would like to get in: If Franklin Delano Roosevelt was such a great president and his programs were so beneficial, how come the twenty second amendment limiting presidential terms to two, was passed about six years after his death in office while his former vice president (Harry S Truman) was still president? Anyway, back to the discussion at hand.

So if we are going to go forward with career politicians, why not get the best ones that money can buy? As much as we like to denounce career politicians, at least the ones that aren't our own representatives, the fact is we are not going to do away with the type of people that we classify as professional politicians. And here's another thought: why should we try? Why not have professional, experienced, talented people looking after the governance of our country? When you hire someone to work at your house, or to carry out some kind of other business for you, is your sole criteria to the exclusion of any other factor, how cheaply they will work? If it is, how does that work out for you?

As far as I can determine, as I write this, the salaries of our United States senators and representatives are something less than two hundred thousand dollars a year. I'm sorry, but no matter what you think of two hundred thousand dollars, that is a paltry amount of money to try and attract mature, smart, sensible people that are at the tops of their professions. We have already invested a couple of centuries in trying the system of getting the best people into government that we can without paying a realistic salary and look where we are now—trillions of dollars in debt, being ruled in all but name by a large, out of control central government, and here is the most important part, struggling to satisfactorily resolve this mess against the wishes of the established federal government rather than with the help or leadership of our elected officials that are supposed to be leaders, instead of pillagers.

Along with this increase in pay, we should also change their benefit package to the same benefits the general public gets. Instead of automatic lifetime retirement, they can and should have exactly the same IRA/401(k) opportunities that are available for their constituents. Instead of a separate health care program (as far as I'm concerned, this should be for all government employees), they can buy their own private (using their salary, not our money) health insurance, or participate in the same government health programs that they vote on for the general public. In short, while I'm proposing that we raise the pay of our congress people, I also want to get rid of all the extra perks that congress has lavishly indulged in over the years. While I'm suggesting that we try to get better people, and pay them what they are worth, I definitely want all of their compensation right out in the open. Encouraging people to feather their nests away from the public eye is a large part of what has brought us to the difficulties we are experiencing now.

Think how much better off we would be right now if the senators and representatives that we are going to have to depend on to carry us through some of the worst problems we have endured since the revolution (more than two hundred and twenty five years ago) were the best of the best. Wouldn't it be better to have people who are the cream of the crop, and have an interest in doing a good job because they are well paid patriots and their main focus is keeping our country in the best shape possible?

Instead, even now, we have a Congress largely run by power seeking progressives that are focused on maintaining their hold on that power. We have of course elected a new freshman class of representatives made up mostly of conservatives and tea party candidates. While I think that's great, and I wish that there were more of them, I feel that hanging all our hopes on the newly elected conservatives is putting a lot of responsibility on them. If we are going to ask them to do everything we want, starting with putting out a health care repeal bill, why don't we go ahead and pay them for it? The new conservatives along with any more that we can elect in 2012 aren't just going to be in a position to do a lot of good; we are depending on them to go against the entrenched bureaucrats and liberals that have been building their power bases for decades. If we are going to start sorting out the chaos we find ourselves in, it would be a lot easier for these new representatives and senators to fight these battles for us if they were well compensated.

I also think it would be much better if we were attracting experienced people who have a history of making money and supporting themselves because that ability to go back to the private sector means that they will have a "fallback position" and will not be held hostage by people who can contribute campaign funds for their potential reelection or by influential people that can "make or break" a political career. In my fevered imaginings, I would like to think that our theoretical well compensated legislator who could still make better money in the private sector, would resist the type of political arm twisting that Nancy Pelosi resorted to in the battle to pass the health care travesty. I don't know if the system that I am proposing will accomplish that, but I do know that the way we do it now isn't getting us enough of the kind of legislators we need.

As much as our federal senators and representatives try to convince us that they work for and are accessible to each and every one of us individually, that just isn't so. It isn't realistic to think that each and every one of us can get personal attention from these people. The number of citizens that they each represent is just too large. Members of the House represent over six hundred thousand people each. In the state I live in, the population is over twenty million. How a reasonable person can expect two senators to represent that many people on a personal level is beyond me. This is something that we (taxpayers and voters) contribute to, since we also like to think that we can directly contact our federal senators and representatives any time we like.

Again, despite our increased involvement, since we must rely on our federal elected officials to often work unwatched, we need ethical, dependable people to fill those positions. In short, what we desperately need is for the people that we elect to high office to take care of running the national government ethically with a focus on doing what is best for the country instead of what's best for the politicians. That way the rest of us can focus on our day to day lives and pay attention to being productive, taxpaying, opportunity using, citizens of the great republic that is the United States of America. To reach that happy state, we are going to have to attract the type of people to office that we can depend on.

As I said earlier, it is very important that we stay in touch with our members of Congress and let them know what we expect but because of the numbers involved, most of this "staying in touch" is going to involve dealing with a staff person who is responsible for handling just this type of contact. I can't count the number of times that people have told me they were unhappy with a senator or representative because they couldn't talk to the person directly, or, and this seems to really set people off, received a form letter back from the particular politician's office. I don't think that a form letter or some kind of brief response means an opinion went unnoticed; I think it just means that the sheer number of contacts has made it impossible to generate a personal response to every call or letter. I feel that what a form letter says is a lot more important than the fact that it isn't a personal note.

So again, if we are going to have people in Congress that we expect to properly attend to both the interests of us as constituents and at the same time the welfare of the entire country, while additionally being basically unsupervised, I think paying enough money to get the best people for these positions is going to turn out to a better use of our money than what is going on right now.

Is raising congressional pay alone going to solve all the issues in front of us? No, of course not. We have a lot of problems that are each and every one going to need well thought out, tough, controversial decisions made by people that are thinking about our country, not their political careers. Pretty much the kind of politicians that are not the majority in Congress right now. There are a lot of factors that go into attracting the people we need and money alone will not do it. I'm merely suggesting that we take one bad condition (low pay) out of the job description and see if we can start getting the best people available for the job.

I realize that suggesting a pay increase for congress people is going to be a very unpopular idea. In fact, that suggestion isn't even the point of this book, or even necessarily this chapter. What I'm trying to point out is that we need to "think out of the box" or at least do things differently. The reason that even mentioning paying better money to politicians is so unpopular is because of the poor quality people that we have been electing. The system that we have been using has brought us Barney Frank, Nancy Pelosi, Harry Reid, Joe Biden, Charles Schumer and Anthony Weiner. Of course nobody wants to give people like that more money. We should be fining them for the awful job that they have done, not offering them a raise. However; the way we do things now attracts just that kind of people. Whatever types of changes it takes to get the honest, ethical, responsible politicians that we need in leadership positions, we desperately need to indentify and make those changes.

If raising the pay of our elected federal politicians will get us the leaders we need, then I think that the money we have saved up to this point by not paying our senators and representatives well, is some of the worst money that we never spent.